The concepts in *Healing th*
in such a way as to make
I found this book to be an enjoyable and interesting read but also
full of story examples and real science. This book was exactly the
resource I needed as one dealing with PTSD myself. It is a must-
read.

—Pastor Jay Alexander
USMC veteran, professional firefighter

I strongly believe in Aaron Quinonez's mission and found his story
engaging, insightful, and eye-opening. God is working in the lives
of veterans, and Aaron's book showcases God's amazing love for the
warriors who defend our great nation.

—Michael Webster
Non-veteran member of Operation Pop Smoke (suicide
prevention program and app)

Healing thru Service offers a life-changing path for those courageous
enough to confront their struggles with PTSD. Motivated by his
own struggles with PTSD, Sgt Q takes readers on a transformative
journey to discover that serving others is key to their own healing.
Aaron's words are not fiction but are truth documented through
personal experience as a Marine combat veteran, in-depth scientific
research, and years of service as a warrior on the front lines in the
battle to help others overcome the destructive impacts of PTSD.
Evident throughout his writing is Aaron's deep faith in God, his
relentless desire to help others, and his willingness to persevere no
matter the cost.

—Colonel Chaplain Scott McChrystal, US Army (retired)
Executive liaison, The Warrior's Journey

Healing thru Service opened doors by showcasing a formula where we all can ground ourselves in the comfort of knowing that God is with us. In this amazing book, Sgt Q is clear when he shared with us how healing takes place. How we are not stuck. How we can move forward by learning, understanding, and loving ourselves. I now know that with positive beliefs, hope is real and transformation is possible. The understanding of our self-image is crucial to becoming an agent of change.

—Ericka E. Kelly, USAF CMSgt (retired)

HEALING
THRU
SERVICE

REDEMPTION
PRESS

HEALING
THRU
SERVICE

THE WARRIOR'S GUIDEBOOK TO OVERCOMING TRAUMA

SGT Q

UNITED STATES MARINE CORPS, 1ST ANGLICO

Published by Redemption Press, PO Box 427, Enumclaw, WA 98022.

Toll-Free (844) 2REDEEM (273-3336)

Redemption Press is honored to present this title in partnership with the author. The views expressed or implied in this work are those of the author. Redemption Press provides our imprint seal representing design excellence, creative content, and high-quality production.

ISBN 13: 978-1-64645-152-4 (Paperback)
978-1-64645-154-8 (ePub)
978-1-64645-153-1 (Mobi)

Library of Congress Catalog Card Number: 2020902125

This book is dedicated to my wife and family, who have endured my healing process and now help me to champion the healing of others through the QMissions ministry.

For all those who are lost in the pain of your past—we are coming to find you.

CONTENTS

INTRODUCTION

These forges, hotter than any other on earth,
set to purify my soul, burn up all impurity to refine me,
though not as silver.
Isaiah 48:10, author's paraphrase

MEMORIAL DAY, A HOLIDAY I SPEND like many other veterans I know, bellied up to a bar drinking cheap beer and shots of whiskey. I order my Jim Beam with sour, and another shot of whiskey and a bottle of Bud Light for my friend and fellow Marine Bryan.

My mind wanders to a time before the war, a time of my youth when Bryan and I spent many a day drinking beer and eating fish and chips. We were barely nineteen, but we were never carded.

Two Marines in uniform in a small town hardly drew the suspicion of the waitstaff. Even if they suspected we were underage, they wouldn't think to ask us for ID. Knowing we were willing to fulfill our duty and put our lives on the line for our country would supersede any conviction of duty to the law they may have felt. There is something almost magical about a hot lightly breaded piece of fish and an ice-cold beer that still sets my mind ablaze with thoughts of a life I once lived, a much simpler life before the war.

The whiskey and beer slide gently across the bar as the bartender hands me my drink. I sit silently sipping my bourbon and watching small beads of sweat form on the surface of the bottle of beer until enough condensation gathers and gravity takes over, pulling the moisture down to a small puddle on the bar top. Half an hour has passed when the sharp bark of the bartender pulls me out of my thoughts. I look at my drink and see I've had several drinks, as three empty glasses sit in front of me. The bartender asks again as he clears my empty glasses, "Your friend gonna make it?" He gestures to the now warm beer and whiskey shot left untouched from where he had placed them next to me a half hour before.

I never look up from my glass, and I say in a low whisper, "Naw, he didn't make it."

I slide off my barstool and slip a fifty onto the bar. The bartender never takes his eyes off me, as he is unsure what to say. I pull Bryan's shot of whiskey to my lips and gulp it down. I feel the warm Tennessee whiskey burn across my tongue and down my throat. The burn in my mouth matches the burn in my eyes as they begin to swell with tears. I set the shot glass inverted on the mouth of the beer bottle and turn to the door. The quick motion and sudden flood of emotions make my head swim, and I fight to maintain my balance as I hasten my pace to exit. I have to get outside before I lose it.

THIS WAS HOW I SPENT THE majority of my Memorial Day holidays. But this year would be different. This year I would be outside CONUS (the continental United States) for the first time since returning from Iraq. This time I would be on mission, but it would be different; I wouldn't be going to fight and bring destruction, but to help and bring hope. I would be traveling to Mexico with a church group to build a house for a homeless family. When I left that day and stepped across the border, I had no idea my life would be forever changed and the life I once knew would be gone in the blink of an eye.

I served in the US Marines, in a Special Forces unit called 1st ANGLICO (Air Naval Gun Liaison Company). During my time there, I received a lot of high-speed training. I became a communications specialist cross-trained as a forward observer, a close combat instructor, a naval weapons security manager, and a master parachutist. We trained for MOUNT (military operations in urban terrain) and had cold-weather training in Bridgeport, California. We had a high OP tempo and spent millions of taxpayer dollars (thank you) in ordnance and jet fuel as we trained to call for fire. With all this specialized training and high-speed gear, I was ready for war. I was ready to take the fight to the enemy. I was ready to rain lightning from the sky and bring thunder from the sea.

It wasn't quite as glorious as I envisioned. With all my specialized, million-dollar training, I mostly sat in the desert on an outpost watching the endless desert, seeing the firefights from a distance, hearing the chatter of those engaged on the radio, and listening to the chaotic sounds of frantic men calling out positions requesting reinforcements of shifting field fire. I experienced the fear and panic in the crackling voice of Doc calling out for help after a young soldier was hit. The sounds of that radio static still haunt me today. I would never again know the life I once knew.

My combat experience was limited in Iraq, and when I returned home, I felt as if I hadn't done enough over there. I felt like I hadn't pulled my weight. I came home feeling less like a hero and more like a fraud. Like an imposter in my uniform.

I began to have nightmares, which turned into sleepless nights. I didn't know what to do as I experienced audible hallucinations and panic attacks. I thought, *No way. Not me. How could I be suffering posttraumatic stress?*

I'd done only one tour with limited combat experience. The PTSD diagnosis felt like I'd received a death sentence. I was terminal, sentenced to a life of mental hospitals and prescriptions. I thought I'd lost my life and lost all hope. I struggled coming to grips with this label and felt like I didn't deserve to have PTSD. That condition was reserved for the real warfighters—the ones who had multiple deployments and Purple Hearts.

The label of PTSD and this false belief held me back for a long time. Even when God called me to start helping other veterans with my testimony, I felt like I couldn't respond because someone with more combat experience should be doing it—someone with real bravado and an impressive war record.

Although it took time, God showed me that even with my limited combat experience, my suffering was real. What God revealed to me turned my world upside down: If I could step out of the shadows of shame and talk about my experiences, it would give courage to others to do the same. It completely shifted the way I thought about my own trauma experiences. My nightmares and the panic, anger, and depression were real; they greatly affected me and had a detrimental impact on my life. So if I was suffering from the effects of war, even with my limited exposure, how much more were those guys with multiple deployments and impressive records suffering?

If I could speak up and say, "Hey, I need help. I'm struggling, but I am surviving," I could motivate my brothers to do the same. They could look at me and see that it's okay to ask for help. By telling my story and sharing my experiences, I could give them hope.

I read a lot, and one of the books that impacted me was *Ameri-*

can Sniper by Chris Kyle. In his book, he said he felt the same way as I did and that he didn't do enough during the war. Chris Kyle, the most decorated warrior of our generation, felt like he didn't pull his weight. How is that possible? I later found out that this is a common lie we all tell ourselves—that someone always had it worse or did more than we did, so our testimony doesn't have as much value.

This mindset isn't limited to the veteran community. Victims of severe childhood abuse often fear coming forward, thinking they won't be believed and that others suffered so much more than they did. They, too, discount their own pain. If I felt I didn't do enough to help my brothers in Iraq, God was showing me the way to provide and help them on their next mission. He would deploy me on a new battlefield, one that claims more lives than the Iraq desert did. In this new war, the battlefield of the mind, hope would become my new ammunition, and the mission field would be the centerpiece of a new battle plan.

After that first phone call from my friend with the invitation to help serve in Mexico and the first mission trip, I traveled the globe for seven years with various missionary organizations. I helped build homes, orphanages, and churches, dig wells, and feed people, all the while spending my own time and money. I did four or more of these trips a year, being deployed from one to three weeks at a time. All the structures we built and all the supplies delivered were simply empty vessels. The true commodity we delivered was hope. Without hope, all the other accomplishments were meaningless. The hope we brought to the people was in fact the same hope I received.

I didn't realize this at first. I just knew that as soon as I returned home, I wanted to be back on a mission. It became a deep yearning in my soul. It took time to realize that I was receiving more from these trips than I was giving. I received healing—I was healing by serving. This was an incredible revelation and only furthered my desire to share my experience with others who were waging similar battles. The model became one of the foundational building blocks for what came to be known as QMissions. The QMissions motto is "Healing thru Service" and has developed into a mantra by which our alumni live out their lives. QMissions is now a platform where veterans can fulfill their God-given mission here on earth.

Through QMissions, an award-winning program was birthed and aptly named Operation Restore Hope. The fundamentals of Healing thru Service became the hammer (literally and figuratively) used to break the cycle for those coping with posttraumatic stress. The program focuses on how the brain operates and uses hope as the guide to create new, positive triggers while in otherwise traumatic surroundings. The mission is run like a boot camp, where all new recruits start right where I started—building a house for a homeless family in Mexico in two days. This process is a pathway for all involved to reset their lives and is a launching pad that uses hope as the guide toward a successful future.

This book has grown out of several years of walking in obedience to the Lord. In the following chapters, I unpack life lessons I've learned along the way that have helped me heal from the effects of war. These hard-fought lessons were taught on the mission fields of the South Pacific in places like Cambodia, Indonesia, and the Philippines; on the vast mission fields of Africa in Swaziland, Malawi, Cape Town, Rustenburg, and Kenya; and on the mission fields of Central and South America in Mexico, Haiti, Honduras, and Brazil. In these places I learned how to fight and be victorious on the greatest battlefield I have ever known: the battlefield of my mind in overcoming PTSD.

The book is a guide for the wandering and lost warrior to the path of healing. It isn't necessary to be a Christian to use the tools in this book, although I believe it would help substantially. Do keep in mind that some of the vernacular is specific to my brothers- and sisters-in-arms—the veterans. These wandering warriors speckle a vast landscape with their presence, yet desire to be forever hidden from society. Even though I'm a veteran writing to veterans and warfighters, there are universal truths that can be of great use and comfort to all those seeking to overcome any trauma they've experienced. At some point, we will all experience trauma and be left with its indelible stain.

Let's take a minute here to clarify the place of women warriors in QMissions and my use of gender-specific terms. When I use terms like brothers-in-arms, I am including the women who serve with us, who are just as valiant and just as well-trained and skilled as their male comrades, and who suffer just as much.

During our time together, I will show you a step-by-step process to overcome your trauma and create a life filled with gratitude, fulfillment, and purpose. Throughout, I will share my stories and adventures overseas that will accentuate each point and help you connect to the concepts we are covering. These are my personal recon. I will reference scientific studies researched as field intel and Scripture passages that relate to the subject matter, because without God's guidance and direction none of this would be possible. In addition, I have added a tactical application section to assist you with ways to process and practice what you learn.

Each chapter will follow a format of an introduction to an idea via personal recon, the facts of the matter generated from field intel, Scripture unpack, tactical application, and then a debrief with a functional check. It will allow for a semblance of repetition and will set the expectation for each chapter. Most people learn best through repetition, so in this way you will gain a better understanding of the material and have a greater chance of success. If you will allow me to be your guide, your mentor, your cadre, and your friend, I promise to do my very best to equip you with the weapons and tactics you need to be victorious on this new emerging battlefield against your most formidable foes, whatever they might be. Together, we can be victorious and join the ranks of the Spirit-filled warriors who have come before us. Through the process of Healing thru Service, I am free from my past pain, and together we can propel ourselves into the greatness that we are destined to achieve.

CHAPTER 1

TOXIC CAMPS

The process is cheap; it will only cost you all you have.
—Sgt Q

Personal Recon

WHEN DID YOU TURN FROM A soldier into a warrior? Was it when you found out there are others just like you? This happens the moment you realize that your brothers-in-arms are just as driven, motivated, and fearless as you—and a bond is formed, forged in the flames of shared adversity. Once the battles with your brothers come to an end and you return home to the lifestyle you left behind, it is a struggle to fit in. You feel like you don't belong in your own country and are out of place, forgotten, disrespected, discarded, and most of all—misunderstood. The harder you try to fit in, the more you feel lost.

Feelings like these troubled me constantly, making me feel like I was alone, and the PTSD would only seek to further isolate me. Oh, how I longed for the nights I could sleep without fear and wake with joy in my heart instead of terror.

> 3:30 a.m. Friday:
>
> Tonight I am at war. War with myself, my body, and with my mind. I went to bed full of worry and stress, and it seeps out of my mind and into my heart. My pulse is racing, my throat is dry and tight. I feel sick to my stomach. It is an uneasy sickness, like a near miss in a car accident, or when that first round breaks the silence of the of the midday heat. It is the gut wrenching feeling something greater than fear. It is the absence of hope that grips our mortality and drags us into the abyss. A dark hole where there is no light, no sound, and no hope. A darkness so black you lose all sense of reality and purpose. No sound but the sound of your own screams deafening in the silence. No hope.
>
> This is hell. The absence of hope. Separation from the light. How did I get here again? (Sgt Q's personal journal)

Stop trying to fit in! It is a myth, and you're never going to be the person you were before. No longer a soldier, you are now a warrior. Likely you didn't fit in before joining the military—that's why you joined. So why would it be any different now? Accept who you are. No! Don't accept it—embrace it, own it, and relish it! Apply the warrior mentality to overcome the new obstacles in your life. Look to the warrior principles of justice, judgment, dependability, integrity, decisiveness, tact, initiative, enthusiasm, bearing, unselfishness, courage, knowledge, leadership, and endurance. These are the hallmarks of a warrior; this is who you are. Odds are these new challenges pale in comparison to those you faced while in the military. The same attributes that brought success in the military will forge a successful warrior of God. The process is cheap; it will only cost you all you have.

Repurpose Your Tactics

The pain you experience is a lens from which you view the world. Emotional pain hurts. It hurts just as bad as physical pain. Emotional pain from trauma causes real physical sensations. To say someone is brokenhearted is a true description. The heart hurts as if it were a bone crushed under the weight of a situation, as if someone had stomped on it and shattered it into a million pieces.

This pain you experience is the lens that can distort your thoughts and turn into destructive actions. When destructive action is practiced, it becomes unfavorable conduct. Unfavorable conduct over time will malign your character and will haunt your life, following your name long after death. Character, conduct, actions, and thoughts can't be changed until the lens you are looking through is identified. Once it is identified, you can change the way you think and feel about past pain.

This pain is holding you back—there is no doubt. The pain, hurt, and trauma that have built up over the years are all pulling like a stone in a slingshot. As the stone gets pulled back in the slingshot, tension builds, and all those things you think are holding you back are only doing so because you have to let them go. Once you decide to release and let go, all the stored-up inertia will then launch you into a future full of hope and purpose. You will soar faster and farther than you ever could imagine.

By altering your perspective about your pain, you release yourself from that which is holding you back, and then you can use it to propel you into a future free from its grasp.

I want to offer encouragement that you can repurpose your military battle tactics to help achieve victory in this internal emerging war. Posttraumatic stress is the new battlefield, and to prepare for this war, new weapons of warfare need to be forged. However, to best this enemy, understanding the terrain is critical. I find that most people hunker down into three different toxic camps when it comes to post-traumatic stress: victim mentality, denial, and the silent majority.

The First Toxic Camp: Victim Mentality

Toxic victim mentality is a minority camp that inflicts our society in general, but it spreads like an infection among the veteran community. It infects our minds and limits our ability to rationally process how we perceive civilian life. As a victim, we hold no personal responsibility for our actions. A victim feels as though they are just the sum of what has happened to them in this world. A victim feels unequipped, unable, and held back from success because of "X." Although "X" may be different for everyone, it has the same result on our psyche. If we're not careful, we can get stuck in a hole of self-pity, blinded by our pain and unable to see the joys that life can bring.

I had good reason to join the ranks of the growing number of those afflicted with this sickness. I had a birth defect that could have confined me to a wheelchair. I nearly drowned as a toddler. I grew up poor, with no running water or electricity until I was ten years old. I had an alcoholic and abusive father. I was homeless. I have posttraumatic stress from my experiences in Iraq. My first marriage ended in divorce. I nearly lost my business because of another's actions, and I faced financial ruin. Yes, any one of those could have been my "X," and I could have relegated myself to a life of self-pity, blaming others for my misfortune.

I was not immune from this sickness, and I lived with this victim mentality for years. I was angry and bitter, blaming everyone else, believing the world owed me something because of the hardships I had endured. I know what it is like to live in the toxic victim mentality camp, to live without hope where the squalor of self-pity stinks of rotten dreams and broken promises. I could have lived the rest of my life there, or I could change my perception from "look what happened to me" to "look what I've overcome."

The Second Toxic Camp: Denial

The camp of denial consists of those who deny the existence of posttraumatic stress or the severity of its effects. In this camp, we hear things like:

"They should just get over it."
"They're weak."
"They're faking it."
"It's not that hard."
"Just buck up."
"If you just tried harder or had more faith."
"People with posttraumatic stress are damaged goods or are dangerous."

These are all cruel phrases used to diminish the anguish of those suffering with this disability. Denial leads to the assumption that all who suffer with this condition are useless and lack the mental fortitude to be successful in life. The denial camp and its perpetuation of wrong stereotypes create a hostile environment for those who struggle with mental illness, and it leads to the further isolation of those who desperately need support and compassion. Life in this camp is defined by those who do not know us or understand, and yet we allow them to dictate a perception of ourselves.

The Third Toxic Camp: The Silent Majority

When it comes to mental health, most of us fall somewhere on the spectrum of the silent majority. We all suffer and cope in different ways and in different degrees. This is part of the complexity of posttraumatic stress. A trigger for some may not be a trigger for others. What we all share is a reservation about asking for help. We all fear being labeled by the denial camp as someone from the victim mentality camp. We don't want to appear weak or have people look down on us with disdain or pity. We suffer in silence, holding on to our pain until it overruns our borders and takes us hostage in our minds. When we choose to keep quiet, we fail on two fronts: first, by doing nothing to change the stereotypes surrounding posttraumatic stress, and second, by failing to give hope to others who are suffering in silence.

Someone must break the silence, step forward, and fight back the fear of judgment. Someone must blaze a new trail and establish a new way of thinking about how to live with posttraumatic stress.

Field Intel

The Mental Health Foundation from the UK has produced many articles and gives access to published studies that show that altruism makes us more mentally fit and increases happiness and quality of life. The research is in, and it looks good for all the "do-gooders" out there changing the world one act of kindness at a time. The data shows that not only the person receiving the act of kindness receives benefit, but the person performing the act of kindness also gets quantifiable positive results from the event. It also creates a sense of community, helping us to not feel isolated, which fights back depression.[1]

Helping others also helps us to keep our lives in perspective, creating hope for our future. This type of experience is contagious,

[1] "What Are the Health Benefits of Altruism?" *Mental Health Foundation*, November 8, 2019, www.mentalhealth.org.uk/publications/doing-good-does-you-good/health-benefits-altruism.

and we will share it with others, expanding the reach of our good deeds. There was a famous study by Harvard in the 1980s that showed that even watching someone else do a good deed yielded benefits to the observer. This is affectionately known as known as the Mother Teresa Effect.[2]

In a simple experiment, 132 students at Harvard University watched a fifty-minute video that showed Mother Teresa carrying out acts of kindness. Saliva swabs were taken from the students before they started watching the video and again immediately afterward. Levels of salivary immunoglobulin A (S-Ig A) were then measured in the swabs. This substance is an important component of the immune system, the first point of defense when a virus, bacteria, or other pathogen gets into your mouth, perhaps through contaminated food.

By the time the film was over, the levels of S-Ig A had risen in the students and were still high an hour later. The researchers suggested this was because the students "continued to dwell on the loving relationships that characterized the film."[3]

If there are quantifiable data sets that prove the health benefits from just being a casual observer of these actions, imagine for a moment how much more benefit there is for the active participant. Think back to a time someone went out of their way to help you with something. How did that make you feel? Have you ever done the same for someone else? If not, today is the day to try it out.

Scripture Unpack

This entire book you are about to read can be summarized in the following verses from Isaiah 58:6–12 (ESV):

---

[2] David R. Hamilton, "Can Kindness Boost the Immune System?" *David R Hamilton PhD: Using Science to Explore*, July 24, 2018, https://drdavidhamilton.com.

[3] David C. McClelland and Carol Kirshnit, "The Effect of Motivational Arousal through Films on Salivary Immunoglobulin A," *Psychology & Health*, 2, no. 1, 1988: 31–52, https://www.tandfonline.com/doi/abs/10.1080/08870448808400343.

Is not this the fast that I choose:
  to loose the bonds of wickedness,
  to undo the straps of the yoke,
to let the oppressed go free,
  and to break every yoke?
Is it not to share your bread with the hungry
  and bring the homeless poor into your house;
when you see the naked, to cover him,
  and not to hide yourself from your own flesh?
Then shall your light break forth like the dawn,
  and your healing shall spring up speedily;
your righteousness shall go before you;
  the glory of the LORD shall be your rear guard.
Then you shall call, and the LORD will answer;
  you shall cry, and he will say, "Here I am."
If you take away the yoke from your midst,
  the pointing of the finger, and speaking wickedness,
if you pour yourself out for the hungry
  and satisfy the desire of the afflicted,
then shall your light rise in the darkness
  and your gloom be as the noonday.
And the LORD will guide you continually
  and satisfy your desire in scorched places
  and make your bones strong;
and you shall be like a watered garden,
  like a spring of water,
  whose waters do not fail.
And your ancient ruins shall be rebuilt;
  you shall raise up the foundations of many generations;
you shall be called the repairer of the breach,
  the restorer of streets to dwell in.

The verses I have laid out here paint a clear picture of our motto at QMissions: Healing thru Service. Let me help you unpack these six verses, as it will help you to understand this book of the Bible and its teachings in a more comprehensive way.

Isaiah 58 is a chapter about fasting and how people would use fasting as a way to quarrel and oppress each other, using the fast to seek after their own pleasures (v. 3). The writer turns fasting on its head as he explains true fasting.

Verses 6 and 7 say that sharing your food with the hungry and bringing the homeless into your house will loose the bonds of the wicked, undo the yoke of bondage, and allow the oppressed to go free. The author says that this is the fasting God chooses. He goes on to say that when we choose this type of fasting, this type of sacrifice and service to the Lord, light will break forth like the dawn, and healing shall spring up speedily (verse 8).

In verses 10 and 11, we are told that when we feed the hungry and help the afflicted, our reward is that our light will shine in the darkness and it will be as bright as noonday; we will be like a spring that does not run dry, and our bones will be made strong.

I take a lot of veterans suffering with trauma onto the mission field to serve others in a way they have never done before. I ask them to sacrifice their time and money to do so. Many are apprehensive to take this step. It is so foreign for them to willingly spend their time and money to build a home for someone they don't know—to take time off work, to fly to another country, and to spend their savings, all to serve someone else and receive no tangible benefit. They are apprehensive at first, but by the end of the mission, the comment I hear most frequently from the team during the debrief is they feel they received much more than they gave to the mission. They share how they were restored with hope and healing and that they will never be the same.

I, too, can attest to this fact of the transformation and the healing. I have experienced every word breathed in these verses. My light has come forth; my healing has been rapid. When I have called on the Lord, He has answered; my light has led others to find healing, my bones have been made strong, and my life is a spring that does not fail. My new hope is that I will be able to live out verse 12—that this book and the teachings in it will build a foundation for future generations of warfighters and trauma suffers, that many will come to know the healing God offers through serving others, and that through our service to God and to others, we will repair the breach and restore the streets we dwell in.

When we live our lives in service to others, we are given a peace that surpasses all understanding. We are blessed beyond measure, healing the pain of our past and causing our light to shine in the darkness, illuminating like it was midday. It is a strange concept, I know, but over the next few chapters I will do my best to unpack this knowledge in a structured way that will lend itself to a greater understanding of how God calls us to live with one another in this world.

Tactical Application

This is a simple activity. Choose to do something small and meaningful for people in your life. Choose to do this for the next week and record your own results. Record your feelings before and after each act, and then revisit them at the end of the week to reconcile the results. You must plan these out because it so easy to get sidetracked and forget. Here is a simple format for you to use:

	Monday	Tuesday	Wednesday	Thursday	Friday
Name					
Activity					
Feelings before					
Feelings after					

Be sure to give details and look at the words you wrote at the end of your own experiment.

Debrief

If we, the silent majority, find our voices and step out of the shadows, we can create a new perception of posttraumatic stress.

We can show the world that you can live a fulfilling, successful life despite posttraumatic stress. The silent majority are police officers, firefighters, and business owners. We are pastors, social workers, and tradesmen. We are loving fathers and husbands, wives and mothers. We are loyal friends and valuable members of our communities.

Speaking out can change the perception of what others think posttraumatic stress looks like in three important ways:

1. It will quell the negative conversation about PTSD when the manner in which we live our lives overturns the stereotypes that plague mental health conditions.
2. We will embolden more of the silent majority to come forward and share their stories. There is power in our testimonies.
3. Most importantly, we will give hope to those who live in the toxic camp of victim mentality and assure them they do not have to stay there. We can help them realize that they, too, can live better lives free from the shame and self-loathing that holds them back.

During our time together in this book, I will enlighten you about what you can look for to broaden your scope and explore new terrain. On the battlefield of the mind, you need a superior strategy, superior weapons, and impenetrable armor. The same as on the battlefield, we need a superior mindset and a superior strategy, and these require preparation and gathering of intel.

CHAPTER 2

STEP OUT OF
THE SHADOWS

Welcome to the funhouse of horrors that is my mind.
—Sgt Q

Personal Recon

HERE IN THIS SECTION, YOU WILL find the innermost thoughts, shocking and true like a horrific murder scene. My brain is filled with clues of the culprit, motive, and accessories to the crime of existing in a broken world. A fallen soldier rising like a phoenix from the ashes, I am still haunted by the flesh of the past, which hangs on like a charred remnant of the former self—not fully alive but not quite dead. Somewhere in the midst of a rebirth, I linger in the sorrow of a former, unable to climb out from where I came. With a grip on my soul, the darkness calls to me.

> Welcome to the funhouse of horrors that is my mind. I live this life. I am in a constant state of flux. Ever changing what I believe to be true and evolving into a more robust version of myself. Never knowing if this version is better than the last, only embracing the new version. There are usually several small shifts in my thinking patterns that will reveal new truth in a way that is gradual, and the new concept is easily absorbed into the reality of my mind. New doors open as old ones close in the understanding of myself and how I operate this meat sack in accordance with social norms. Other times I am stuck in a belief pattern that I believe is a fundamental truth, unwilling to change course in the patterns of thought that are ingrained in my mind. (Sgt Q's personal journal)

At these times it is wise to seek the counsel of someone trusted and senior to you in every way, a person who has already experienced transformation and healing. Once the question is posed and the arguments of each side are exposed, you have a choice to either stay in the truth of your old thought patterns or to evolve into creating a better reality by building a new neural pathway.

This is a difficult process, as many are unwilling to give up their old way because it has often served them well and kept them alive or successful or any number of things you could interject at this point. At these junctures I have learned to always seek to evolve. I make a conscious effort to accept the new reality as truth, discarding the old truth. It is not that the old truth was a lie or incorrect; it was correct for its time, but now serves no other purpose but to stunt my growth. Like the phoenix spreading its wings to capture oxygen, the fuel needed to burn off the old self and shake off the remnants of its former life.

My mind feels like it grinds to a halt as it shifts direction into a willingness to accept a new version of reality that was not concluded by myself through a long process of study and discovery. This shift is more dramatic and often painful and scary as you willingly give up your version of reality to embrace another.

For me, I need twenty-four to seventy-two hours of processing time to fully delete and then upload the new reality of my thought process. Like an update for your computer, the mind must shut down all other processes to focus 100 percent of its power on deleting the old, buggy OS and uploading the new one. This process often leaves me in a state of disbelief, unwilling at times to let go of the old to embrace the new. It is a unique experience because you betray the former version of yourself to accept the reality of another.

Now, do you open your eyes to the global truth known to those who have been enlightened, to realizing your thought process and version of an incorrect reality? Or do you simply embrace another version of reality and make it your own? Of this I am not sure, but on either account, it is acceptable for the transformation to take place, at first with a willingness to accept the new reality without actually, fully believing it to be true. That is a strange conclusion, I know, but it is a most valuable one, I assure you.

To stay alive, I must continue to grow into a better version of myself. The painful process of death to self and rebirth in Christ is not an easy onetime event, but is a lifelong journey of self-discovery and renewal of the mind.

For those attempting this journey, I sternly warn you. If you think you have arrived at some form of enlightenment and linger to bask in its glory, you are failing at the very thing you think you are accomplishing. Never be content with where you are. This is a trick of the enemy to stall your growth and distort your identity in Christ. This is a battle; therefore, the rules of war apply: If you aren't taking ground, you are losing it. If you aren't improving yourself and shedding the pain of your past reality, then you are falling back into it. Too much of this for too long will harden your heart and mind, and like the phoenix, your wings will grow tired so you cannot fly.

To make it here and to survive on this new battlefield of the mind, you must be in a constant flux of growth and renewal.

When it is quiet.

When it is dark.

When you are alone.

The stillness of the night is a beautiful thing, the land cloaked in darkness with only the shimmer of the twinkling stars and crescent moon casting shadows across the open fields. The light brings an eerie sense of calm, followed by foreboding thoughts of the unknown. The earth and its creatures are asleep. There are no dogs barking, no birds chirping. Just quiet. The beasts of the field and birds of the air have all tucked themselves safely away for the night. Each scurried away to their safe place, hidden away from the dangers of the night.

Oh yes, there are dangers. You see, predators come out to hunt at night. As the prey lie safely in their dens, the enemy is hunting them, edging ever closer to their hideaway. The cool, still air gives the predators relief from the heat of day, and thus they can endure a lengthy stalk of their game. The blanket of darkness cloaks their movements and masks their approach. They can move stealthily through the fields and forest undetected by their prey, a violent game of cat and mouse. For if they don't hunt, they don't eat, and if they do not eat, they will die. It is not the predators' fault. They are designed this way—to hunt and thin the herd.

In my life I have been both predator and prey, sometimes in the same moment. I would sit for hours at an outpost looking across the vastness of the desert or peering into the darkness of the night.

The anticipation of enemy contact was always looming. It consumes your mind. There is nothing to do out there but wait for the enemy to come. It is a strange and eerie thing to hunt a man. It goes against the very nature of your soul. To watch the last few breaths leave his body, the low guttural growl as life retreats to death—these memories never fade. As his soul escapes this plain of existence, all that is left is the sweet, sickening smell of flesh and blood spilled on the earth. As he expires, a small part of you dies as well—a piece of you that will never come back. Your heart is broken, your soul is wounded, and your mind is shattered.

The unlucky, the lucky, and the foolish. The unlucky freeze, caught in the moment, caught in their mind, unable to escape. They quickly assume the same fate. The lucky ones move forward until they can unpack and process the moment. But the foolish push it down until they can no longer tolerate the memories haunting their existence.

The still of the night can catch me off guard at times. Why, I do not know. There doesn't seem to be a specific trigger; it's just a quiet stillness in the dark of the night. It's like being startled awake or startled when you're relaxing and the rush of fear runs over you. For a brief moment it may feel as if I never left Iraq. I quickly catch my breath and assess the situation, trying to put my mind at ease.

You are home; you are safe. But are you really? Let's just check the security cameras real quick. Better check the perimeter and door locks and windows too while you are up. All these things I say to myself as I begin my rigorous safety behaviors, or compulsions, as the doctor likes to call them. With the house secure, it's off to bed, but there will be little sleep tonight.

The shot of adrenaline that just raced through my body like a freight train has set my mind on fire. Intrusive thoughts and hypervigilance are packed on that train, the one that derailed moments ago.

You know the drill: Breathe. Use your function check.

Sometimes it works, sometimes not. All I know for sure is that it's gonna be a long night. But with the breaking of dawn comes a new day and new hope for a restful night.

At this point in my life, I know that these things will never go away. I just have to learn to live with them. I have to learn to cope with the bad days so there are fewer of them.

Field Intel

When they had a reason to keep swimming—they did.
They did not give up, and they did not go under.
—Curt Richter

In the 1950s, Curt Richter, a Johns Hopkins professor, conducted a gruesome experiment with domesticated and wild rats. He wanted to see if the wild or domestic rat would survive longer when submerged in water. He first took a dozen domesticated rats, put them into jars half filled with water, and watched them drown. The idea was to measure the amount of time they swam before they gave up and went under.

The first rat, Richter noted, swam around excitedly on the surface for a very short time, then dived to the bottom, where it began to swim around, nosing its way along the glass wall. It died two minutes later. The wild rats, renowned for their swimming ability, also swam for about two minutes before eventually giving up and subsequently dying. Both the domestic and wild rats died in much the same way. "What kills these rats?" he wondered.[4]

Richter modified the experiment: He took other, similar rats and put them in the jar. Just before they were expected to die, however, he picked them up, held them a little while, and then put them back in the water. Surprisingly, the rats did not die within minutes

---

[4] Joseph T. Hallinan, "The Remarkable Power of Hope," *Psychology Today*, Sussex Publishers, May 7, 2014, https://www.psychologytoday.com/us/blog/kidding-ourselves/201405/the-remarkable-power-hope.

like the rest. They swam, sometimes for days, before succumbing to exhaustion and dying. What saved the rats? The answer, in a word—hope. Hope of rescue.

In his conclusion, Richter wrote:

> In this way the rats quickly learn that the situation is not actually hopeless.
>
> This small interlude made a huge difference. The rats that experienced a brief reprieve swam much longer and lasted much longer than the rats that were left alone. They also recovered almost immediately. When the rats learned they weren't doomed, the situation wasn't lost, and there might be a helping hand—in short, "when they had a reason to keep swimming—they did. They did not give up, and they did not go under.
>
> After elimination of hopelessness, the rats do not die.[5]

What is hope? How do we find it? How do we hold on to it? If you're a Christian, you know what hope is. Hope is in the Lord Jesus Christ and in the Bible, in truth-talk.

Dr. Gregory Jantz, depression specialist and founder of The Center: A Place of HOPE, says:

> One of the ways to recognize, promote, and sustain optimism, hope, and joy is to intentionally fill our thoughts with positive self-talk.
>
> Too often, the pattern of self-talk we've developed is negative. We remember the negative reactions we were told as children by our parents, siblings, or teachers. We remember the negative reactions from other children that diminished how we felt about ourselves. Through-

---

[5] Hallinan, "The Remarkable Power of Hope."

out the years, these messages have played over and over in our minds, fueling our feelings of anger, fear, guilt, and hopelessness.

One of the most critical avenues we use in therapy with those suffering from depression is to identify the source of these messages and then work with the person to intentionally "overwrite" them. If a person learned as a child he was worthless, we show him how truly special he is. If while growing up a person learns to expect crises and destructive events, we show her a better way to anticipate the future.[6]

QMissions has developed a successful program doing the very same thing. We show people that despite their disability, past, regrets, sins, childhood, or failures, there is hope, and they can find healing. For the purposes of this book, we will call these things "X." We embrace the fact that despite your X, you can still make a difference in the world. Our process of Healing thru Service has received multiple awards from the Washington State Department of Veterans Affairs based on the success of the program and evidence in the lives of the veterans we serve. Sgt Q was named Seattle's Hometown Hero in 2017 for recognition of his faithful service to veterans.

Scripture Unpack

For the weapons of our warfare are not carnal but mighty
in God for pulling down strongholds.
2 Corinthians 10:4 NKJV

We have established from the rat experiments at John Hopkins University that hope is powerful. It allows us to go further than we

[6] Gregory L. Jantz, "The Power of Positive Self-Talk," *Psychology Today*, May 16, 2016, https://www.psychologytoday.com/us/blog/hope-relationships/201605/the-power-positive-self-talk.

ever thought possible, to endure more, and to overcome great odds.

When we look at Scripture, we can see that hope carried the greatest heroes through the toughest times. Hope kept Joseph alive during his time in prison. Wrongly accused and sold as a slave, he never lost hope in the promise God gave him. Hope kept Moses and Aaron motivated as they led the Israelites out of Egypt and into the land God promised for His people. A great hope it must have been, because they wandered in the desert for forty years with people grumbling behind them every step of the way.

The most well-known story about hope has to be the story of David, a shepherd boy with a promise to be king proclaimed by the prophet Samuel. David was the smallest of his brothers and was overlooked by many, but he kept hold of the hope of becoming king. As a young boy, he was sent to fight the mighty giant Goliath. It's possible the promise of becoming king was the hope he held on to as he stepped into battle. Even as King Saul pursued him and marked him for certain death, David held on to the hope God had given him to become the great ruler of Israel. Hope in God's divine providence kept David going in the darkest of times.

Not all of David's problems came from outside influences. There was a time when he was the author of his own demise. When he committed adultery with Bathsheba and then murdered her husband to cover his sin, he created a no-win scenario for himself. David violated the law and, most importantly, God's trust. The pending consequences caused him to become distraught. It was foretold by the prophet Nathan that the son conceived from David's sin would surely die (2 Samuel 12). Spending time in fervent prayer and fasting before the Lord, David continued to repent until he was given word that his son had died.

David found himself in a very dark place (2 Samuel 12:16–23). He had committed adultery and murder, and now because of his sin, his son was dead. Everyone knew what he had done, and the consequences were public. He must have felt very small at this point—defeated and embarrassed, ashamed and distraught over the position he had put himself in. If it were me, I would have wanted to disappear or run away, to hide in the hills in hopes that others would forget about me and my iniquities. Each of us has likely felt this way because of the things we've done or failed to do. All of us have different degrees of regret over the way we've lived our lives. Whether in combat or stateside, we all have things we wish we could change.

Like David, you will have to lament over what you have done or not done. Forgiving yourself and accepting forgiveness from God is the first step. I am sure David, like most of us, wished he could go back and rewrite the past. He spent several days praying and fasting, asking forgiveness with the hope God would spare him from the consequences of his actions. God did not. God allowed him to endure the hardship he caused by his own hand. However, from that hardship came something remarkable, something that perplexed his servants.

After his son's death, David got up, dusted himself off, and moved forward (2 Samuel 12:18–23). He did not wallow in the mindset of regret and sorrow. He did not harbor anger at God. He did not begrudge God for not rescuing him from the consequences. He never lost hope in the promises of God. He knew God would give him another son, another heir to the throne, so he held on to that promise and used it to comfort his wife in her time of grief. Once he realized there was nothing he could do to change the past, David left his sin and regret behind on the floor of the temple where he worshiped God and held tight to His promises. He knew God's promise brought hope. We can follow David's example. We can repent for our sins, but there comes a time when we need to leave them on the floor of the temple, worship, and move forward. We need to release ourselves from the pain and regret of our past and move forward with hope, standing on the promises of God.

We all have greatness inside us birthed through hope. God gave all people in the Bible incredible hope for their future through the coming Messiah, Jesus Christ. It was the hope of a life with meaning and purpose—a life defined by salvation through the sacrifice of Jesus on the cross at Calvary. The same hope we freely receive is the same hope we are commanded to carry forward to the next wanderer. The hope God gave David was for a son who would rule after him and be a strong man of integrity to build a temple for the Lord. Not only did God fulfill His promise, but the Messiah descended through the same bloodline. The second son of David and Bathsheba, Solomon, would be in the lineage of Jesus (Matthew 1:6).

David's story didn't end with Bathsheba, and your story doesn't end here either. You, too, will create a legacy for generations to come.

To understand the battle, we must understand the battlefield we fight on. We know about the physical one. Now let's look at the invisible one.

The Unseen Spiritual Battlefield

When we hold tight to hope and the promises of God, we can endure any hardship or trial that comes our way. But first, we must change our mindset from responding only to the things we see to the things that are unseen. We all know about the warfare on earth, but to be truly victorious, we also have to know about the warfare in the spiritual realm. In fact, the Bible teaches that our real battle is not with flesh and blood, but with powers we do not see but which Jesus Christ came to overcome (Ephesians 6:12).

The first is our sinful nature, which we cannot overcome by ourselves. The second is the unseen world of dark spiritual powers of evil and deception: "For we do not wrestle against flesh and blood, but against principalities, against powers, against the rulers of the darkness of this age, against spiritual hosts of wickedness in the heavenly places" (Ephesians 6:12 NKJV).

In 2 Corinthians 10:3–6 (NKJV), the Bible teaches us to direct our warfare against spiritual strongholds that frequently manifest in our mind:

> For though we walk in the flesh, we do not war according to the flesh. For the weapons of our warfare are not carnal, but mighty in God for pulling down strongholds, casting down arguments and every high thing that exalts itself against the knowledge of God, bringing every thought into captivity to the obedience of Christ, and being ready to punish all disobedience when your obedience is fulfilled.

Once your thoughts are shaped by God's Word, you become fully aware of the battlefield we fight.

The Battlefield of the Mind

There is another very personal battlefield that is part of the spiritual battlefield—it's the battlefield of our mind, and these battles are won and lost with our ideas, beliefs, thoughts, and words. The Bible tells us to be transformed by the renewing of our minds, and it offers new weapons for the process (Romans 12:2).

What are these new weapons? We find some of them in Ephesians 6:10–18 listed as the armor of God. As we walk with our new armor, we are empowered by the Holy Spirit. God helps us to take down strongholds in our minds, such as the deceptions we labor under and the high tower that guards the hurt and pain we can't let go. What are some of these arguments we must cast down?

The MacArthur Study Bible explains it this way:

> Thoughts, ideas, speculations, reasoning, philosophies, and false religions are the ideological forts in which men barricade themselves against God and the gospel. Only through relentless study of the Bible and the precepts of

God, will you be able to reinforce your mind and create a new warrior self, holy and sanctified by God through the sacrifice of Jesus Christ.[7]

MacArthur is explaining the argument to the reader. So perhaps it is a good time to ask yourself, "What arguments am I posing to myself that are causing me strife? What thoughts or regrets am I allowing to steal my joy, cause me pain, and derail my days?" Remember these things as we move to the next section.

Tactical Application

Positive self-talk is not self-deception.
—Gregory L. Jantz

Let's look at how we put into action the things we just learned. Dr. Jantz tells us, "You may have a negative message that replays in your head every time you make a mistake."[8] The first negative message I had to overcome was the feeling that my service was not enough. Yours might be different. As a child, you might have been told, that you would never amount to anything or you couldn't do anything right.

When you make a mistake—and you will, because we all do— you can choose to overwrite that message with a positive. These can be messages such as "I choose to accept and grow from my mistakes" or "As I learn from my mistakes, I am becoming a better person." During this exercise, mistakes become opportunities to replace negative views of who you are with positive options for personal enhancement.

Positive self-talk is not self-deception. It is simply choosing not to mentally look at circumstances with eyes that see only what you want to see. Positive self-talk is about recognizing the truth in sit-

---

[7] John F. MacArthur, editor, exposition on the word *arguments* in 2 Corinthians 10:5, *MacArthur Study Bible*, Harper Collins, 1997.
[8] Jantz, "The Power of Positive Self-Talk."

uations and in yourself. The best kind of positive talk to oneself is what the Bible teaches.

Okay, there it is right there—the negative distorted lens that is shaping the thoughts and actions of the individual. The lens of never amounting to anything and can't do anything right is the lens that distorts the thoughts and drives the destructive behavior. If left unchecked, it can have a detrimental effect on your life.

As a Marine, creating a target list was something I would do as a forward observer. I would survey the battlefield and account for all enemies and positions in our area of operation. I would take note of them and their placement, work up a grid, and create call-for-fire missions for all of them. Then I would wait for our opportunity to take them out with close air support of artillery. Like a giant game of whack-a-mole, we would rain fire down on them when they would pop their heads up to attack. We can use this same tactic to destroy the negative messages we tell ourselves, as well as what the devil tries to challenge us to believe.

How do we discover our lens of pain and change the way we think about it? Don't worry if you are at a loss; I will help you out. For now, I want you to attempt to complete these three steps:

Step 1. Identify your own negative message.
Step 2. Change the conversation in your head.
Step 3. Use this new weapon (truth conversation) anytime this negative lens comes up.

Okay, here's the strategy: Identify a target (negative thought) and work up a fire mission (change the conversation). Then when a negative thought pokes its head up and attacks, you are more prepared with your new weapon—your positive, biblical confrontation.

Function Check

As you read through this book and discover new things about yourself, keep a journal. In this journal, write quick notes that will help you track your thoughts, feelings, and emotions. You will start to discover things about yourself that you didn't know. We at QMissions call this a function check.

In the military, you do a function check when a weapons system is malfunctioning. It's a rapid process of dissecting the weapon's operating system to find the malfunction so you can get back in the fight. Our personal function check is no different. It's designed to narrow down our thoughts, feelings, and emotions through a process of elimination until we can identify the malfunctioning areas in our processing.

Writing in a journal, praying about it, and spending some time figuring this out will help you overcome several destructive conversations in your life. Go ahead and write them all down so you can attack them one by one as you develop the skills necessary to be successful. Like an ANGLICO call for fire, it takes practice and patience to become effective on the battlefield.

This is only day one. Lace up your boots—let's go! We'll go more in-depth into this process in the "SOS: Stuck on Stupid" and "Change Your Thinking, Change Your Life" chapters.

Debrief

You can't see a mental wound, so it's more difficult to heal. It's far easier to recognize a physical wound. Stay with me. We are about to make a fundamental shift in your brain housing group. If we look at a mental wound the same way we look at a physical wound, we can easily create a treatment plan. A physical wound will have to be treated and cleaned. The foreign debris must be separated from the flesh, and the wound needs to be bandaged and protected and given time to heal. If we simply cover it up without treating it properly, it will get infected, cause severe pain, and can go septic and eventually kill us.

The same can be said for a mental wound. We must treat it and clean it. That means unpacking it, talking about it, and separating the truth from the lies we tell ourselves. We will have to bandage it and give the mental wound time to heal. If we simply ignore it, it will lead to severe depression and suicidal ideations, and in too many cases, it will kill us.

Another important thing to remember is to effectively communicate with others about our wounds. I know—scary, right? But what happens if we don't tell others we're wounded? Every time someone brushes up against the wound, the pain will cause us to have a reaction. The offending party won't know why, because the wound wasn't disclosed and we didn't communicate we were hurting. The same can be said of our mental wounds. If we don't tell people we have them, and if we don't tell others what our triggers are, then they won't know how to avoid provoking them and how to help us when we're struggling with them.

CHAPTER 3

SUB VS. CON:

HOW THE BRAIN WORKS

We don't need to learn how to deal with posttraumatic
stress; we need to unlearn it.
—Sgt Q

Personal Recon

WHILE I WAS IN THE MARINES, I was stationed at Camp Pendleton, just a short drive from Pasadena, where my grandmother lived. As often as I could, I would drive up to visit her. She lived alone in a simple one-bedroom apartment within walking distance from all she needed. She was well into her seventies at this point. Her small frame and short stature made her frail in my mind, but her years of raising five kids as a single mother and working as a nurse made her tough and resilient. One of the best parts about going to visit her was she always had fresh tortillas waiting. We would eat them with every meal, and she would always make me a dozen or so to take back to the base with me. Man, were they good in the morning, warmed up with butter smeared across them! Hmm! Often, I would skip breakfast at the chow hall and just eat the tortillas she had prepared.

I can remember one time when I went to visit, and she asked me to get something from the fridge as she was busy pounding out the dough for my batch of tortillas. As I opened the door, the pale light of the fridge came on, and glistening on the shelf was a six-pack of Corona in small, skinny bottles set in their cardboard holder. I was a bit surprised that my little Catholic grandma would have beer in her fridge. I decided to tease her about it.

"Oh, Grandma, what are you doing with this beer in the fridge?" I ribbed her.

"Oh, I got that for you, *mijo*," she said without missing a beat.

"Really? Then why are there two missing?" I inquired.

"Oh, you know," she replied with a chuckle while she kept on beating the dough.

This memory still overshadows all other memories of my grandmother, and I still make her tortilla recipe whenever she crosses my mind. Why is this memory so powerful? Because it is something my brain categorizes as out of the ordinary, surprising. It did not quite fit into the rest of the memories I have of my grandmother, so it stuck out to me. Trauma memories are similar in that they do not fit into the rest of our experiences, so they are sinisterly more problematic.

To understand the concepts laid out in this book, it is helpful to understand how the brain works—well, as best as we can, anyway. Our brain is a complex neural network that allows us to experience and interact with our environment. Our brain constantly makes connections between those things we encounter in our environment and those things it has already learned and categorized. The more experiences we have, the more connections it makes. The more repetitions we experience, the stronger those connections become. Your brain works like a spiderweb, connecting thoughts and experiences from your past to help make sense of your current reality. The brain categorizes memories and experiences, connecting similar experiences and emotions to form a concept of reality—a worldview. We shape this reality through our past experiences, which allow us to make improved, well-informed decisions about the future. The brain's primary focus is our continued survival, so these neural pathways create a blueprint for future decisions based on past experiences.

I'm going to challenge you to put aside what you know about posttraumatic stress. We don't need to learn how to deal with posttraumatic stress; we need to unlearn it.

Here is a simple example most can relate to. You see a commercial where a grandmother is making cookies. So, do that now. Think of cookies. Pause for a moment and recall memories of cookies. Some of you may have fond memories of your grandmother baking cookies when you were little, which may lead to more thoughts and memories about your grandmother—like the summer you spent visiting her at her house where she taught you how to bake. As you reminisce about those memories, you feel joy and warmth and want this for your own family, so you try and remember Grandma's recipe for those cookies. Then you make them for your kids. These thoughts, emotions, and actions are produced from a single second of a commercial. Your brain saw cookies. "Hey, we like cookies!" says the brain; then the brain searches its data banks for cookie memories.

The most powerful experiences of your past transfer from your storehouse of memories to the conscious mind where you recall the emotions related to those memories. This memory data helps us make relevant decisions based on our current and future situations.

Now consider this for a moment: Have you ever tried to share an experience like this with your family, but they just don't get it? You baked the cookies for your kids, and they didn't seem to care as much. Why? You shared a very special moment with them; you recreated the cookies your grandmother made. But, you see, they don't have the same background of experience that you do, so they don't have the same neural network of emotions. They're not the same individual you are.

In contrast, if you shared these cookies with a sibling who was with you when Grandma made the original cookies, then you will have a similar shared experience. You wouldn't have to explain the value of the recipe. You probably wouldn't have to say a word to them. The moment they smelled or tasted the cookies, the shared experience would come rushing back to them, and you would see the expression of joy on their face as their brain began to recall data from their bank of memories. The conversation might go something like this:

> "Oh, these are Grandma's cookies. I haven't had these in years."
>
> "I haven't made them in years either. I wasn't sure if I still remembered the recipe."
>
> "Do you remember how she used to . . ."
>
> "And she would always let us help with . . ."
>
> "Oh, remember the summer she taught us the recipe, and we got to make them on our own?"

Maybe it wasn't cookies your grandma made; maybe it was pasta or sweet tea. My favorite memory of my grandmother is not cookies; it's tortillas. Regardless, the complex neural network connection of memories is the same. It's these shared experiences that draw us closer to one another. The same applies to soldiers who build bonds based on their battle experiences. Soldiers don't have to explain all the details to each other because they each have a neural network that fills in all the gaps and emotions that come with those sensory triggers and memories from the battlefield. Not having this bond with the rest of society is the primary reason we feel like we don't fit in when we come back from serving and try to assume a civilian life.

Field Intel

The memory storehouse has no reasoning skills. It cannot decipher the info as positive or negative.
—Sgt Q

Okay, let's break this down. How does this work? How does the brain recall these memories, and how do emotions get attached to them? Let's look at the brain as having two primary components: the conscious and the subconscious.

The conscious mind is responsible for thinking, planning, analyzing, and decision-making. It receives information from the subconscious mind and has to decide what to do with it. Sometimes it just dismisses the information as nonsense and sends it back to the subconscious to file it away into the nonsense folder. Other times, the conscious mind will make a decision based on the information. A simple example is when it's too hot in the car. The subconscious mind, which regulates body temperature, sends a signal to the conscious mind, making it aware of the temperature. The conscious mind will then decide the best course of action and apply it to the situation. This information is then returned to the subconscious mind, which will process and file it for review in the future. Of course, this is a rather mechanical view of this amazing process, but you get the picture.

When my wife is driving, she likes to have the heat on high with the fan blasting at full speed. My body prefers a much cooler temperature. The subconscious mind will relay to the conscious mind that the temperature in the car is uncomfortable. The conscious mind then has to make a decision about what to do. It looks for options, of which four are available, so the conscious mind must choose one: turn down the temperature, turn down the speed of the fan, open a window, or do nothing. As it contemplates the outcome of each of the four different choices, it relies on the subconscious mind to provide any information on the possible outcomes based on previous experiences.

In the past, turning down the heat or turning off the fan both resulted in an argument with my wife. Noted; next option.

Doing nothing to change the temperature in the past has resulted in the subconscious mind flipping the switch and causing an amygdala hijack, or panic attack. Not good; next option.

Roll down the window. In the past, this has not resulted in an argument, and it has simultaneously cooled down my body temperature. Good option! I roll down the window. The subconscious may also provide additional information. For instance, putting your arm out the window will increase the bare surface area exposed to the rushing wind. From previous experience and experimentation, I know that this will cool the body at a rapid pace. I can then decide to dismiss this information or to implement it to my current behavior.

The conscious mind also solves complex problems, such as planning out our day, fixing an engine problem, and open-heart surgery. The conscious mind derives a plan by accessing all previous experiences and knowledge it has accumulated and stored in the subconscious mind.

The subconscious does most of the busy work. It regulates all your essential body functions, such as breathing, circulation, digestion, and so forth, based upon sensory input. We don't have to think about the things it regulates because the processes are automatic. The subconscious mind gathers the intel, filters the information, and presents it to the conscious mind. The subconscious has no way of making sense out of it or of seeing reality. Once it receives, sorts, and categorizes the information it accumulates in its library of sensory experiences, the subconscious then submits that intel to the conscious mind, which will then process that data to formulate an action plan that your body can execute.

For example, if you were to get too close to the edge of a cliff, you'd begin to feel uneasy. The subconscious mind, the area where past learning is stored, is sending warnings to the conscious mind to stay back because of impending danger. If you continue forward, you might become paralyzed with fear because the subconscious mind has flipped a switch sending you into freeze mode.

The conscious mind, not the subconscious, is the seat of reasoning skills. In the cliff-edge example, the "fear of the edge" alert was intended to prevent certain death, but if you were base jumping and the goal was to go past the edge, then the conscious mind would dismiss the alert and tell the subconscious, "We're okay; we have a parachute." When fear is the connection our subconscious mind makes, the effects can be devastating. Outbursts of anger and rage can overwhelm you because you sense impending doom or death and get debilitated by emotional overloads.

> Edges are dangerous → fall from the edge → fall happens → death possible → Afghanistan → cliffs → Afghanistan cliff memory → death → memories of Afghanistan and Iraq traumas . . . = PANIC

If we don't enter new data into the subconscious, it will continue to bombard us with dated intel.

Here is something to process: Would you send your brothers into a battle scenario based on intel that was months, weeks, or even days old? Take all the time you need with that one.

Scripture Unpack

If our conversations and the words we say to others can
have a profound effect on them, what about the things we
say to ourselves?
—Sgt Q

The Bible teaches that the power of life and death is in the tongue. The things we say, the words we use, can cut people to the bone or raise them up like the wings of an eagle. Do you want to cut people down or help them soar? When we speak rashly, or out of emotion, we allow the subconscious mind to override our reasoning mind. This can often cause strife in our relationships. Proverbs 12:18 (NKJV) says, "There is one who speaks like the piercings of a sword, but the tongue of the wise promotes health." Proverbs 18:21 (NKJV) says, "Death and life are in the power of the tongue, and those who love it will eat its fruit."

Now let us break down this concept. The two verses highlight the way we can use our words and the effects they have on others. The Bible calls our words a piercing sword that can cause death. When we look at the two verses together, we can see a whole new picture evolve as the Scriptures come to life. We see that our words are a powerful weapon God has given us. Like all weapons of war, we must handle them with care, or we may hurt those around us unintentionally.

Do we take care with the words we use? I'm reminded of a gun safety rule we learned in boot camp: Don't point a weapon at anything we don't intend to shoot. Take note about the intent of our words so we don't kill each other spiritually. In contrast, we can kill each other physically with the words we speak to one another. Yes—our words can kill someone physically. Look at the high rate of suicide in our world. People are ending their lives in record numbers due to abuse, bullying, and the torment they experience from others, often from the words spoken against them.

After years of relentless bullying by classmates, thirteen-year-old Rosalie Avila of Yucaipa, California, decided to take her own life. The teenager hanged herself, leaving behind a note apologizing to her parents for the pain she knew her death would cause them. "Sorry, Mom and Dad. . . . Sorry, Mom, that you're going to find me like this."[9]

Unfortunately, this story isn't an isolated incident—it's an epidemic sweeping through this generation. We've all been educated in the English language, but we haven't all been instructed in the power our words possess. Per a British study, nearly half of teen suicides have a direct correlation to bullying.[10] So yes—when we speak to others, our words have a profound effect.

Be mindful of your words. James 3:1–12 goes in depth when it comes to the power of the tongue. James 3:8 (NKJV) says, "No man can tame the tongue." In other words, it has to be controlled.

I use this example of teen suicide to drive home two points. First, the words we say to others have power. I pose the question, though: How much more powerful are the words we speak to ourselves? In the next few chapters, we'll explore this in detail. For now, take a moment to consider the possibility that the words, thoughts, and feelings we are consciously experiencing will have a lasting effect on us physically, mentally, and emotionally.

Second, suicide is not just a veteran issue. It's a systemic problem facing our society today. With the influx of social media, it has become even more prevalent. The ability to hide behind a computer screen and say things you would never say in person has emboldened many to relentlessly torment others with little consequence. Gone are the days of schoolyard bullies getting a beatdown for running off at the mouth. Now they are safely hidden on the internet away from the physical dangers of the venom they spew.

---

[9] https://www.nbcnews.com/news/us-news/bullying-drove-13-year-old-rosalie-avila-kill-herself-parents-n826281.

[10] https://www.independent.co.uk/news/uk/home-news/research-finds-bullying-link-to-child-suicides-1999349.html.

The truth is that the number of suicides is on the rise for most demographics. My hope is that you will take what you learn here and help someone else by sharing this information.

Our words can also bring health and life to those around us. How often does a kind word or a sincerely given "thank you" brighten your day? A Harvard study concluded that people need a six-to-one ratio of positive over negative feedback to be productive.[11] How often do you consciously try to uplift and speak life to others? It seems easier to tear each other down. Therefore, we must train and condition our minds to do the former. Making a concerted effort to use our words in an edifying manner brings life to others. Like any skill we choose to learn, we must practice it. The formula for success with anything is this:

Consistency + Time = Success

We will cover this and a three-step system in later chapters to make this goal much more attainable.

The Fruit of Our Words

Those are the basics, but it gets deeper. The second part of Proverbs 18:21(NKJV) says, "And those who love it will eat its fruit." This fruit is mentioned in the previous verses. Proverbs 18:20 (NKJV) says, "A man's stomach shall be satisfied from the fruit of his mouth; from the produce of his lips he shall be filled." Proverbs 12:14 says (NKJV), "A man will be satisfied with good by the fruit of his mouth, and the recompense of a man's hands will be rendered to him." Both verses equate the words we speak to physical production and the fullness of our bodies.

The words we speak affect not only those around us, but they impact us on a level we cannot see, but feel. We simply need to

[11] Jack Zenger and Joseph Folkman, "The Ideal Praise-to-Criticism Ratio," *Harvard Business Review*, March 15, 2013. https://hbr.org/2013/03/the-ideal-praise-to-criticism.

take the time to notice. If our conversations and the words we say to others can have a profound effect, what about the things we say to ourselves?

I will say this again so you don't miss it. If our conversations and the words we say to others can have a profound effect, what about the things we say to ourselves? How do the things we say and think about ourselves affect our mental and emotional state?

The Bible tells us that our words have power and must be wielded with respect and care—something science is just now understanding.[12]

Tactical Application

I had to allow myself and others into my head to identify
the triggers that created my pain.
—Sgt Q

Now we know about the subconscious mind and the purpose to recall relevant information for the conscious mind to examine. We recognize that our words can have a profound effect on us physically and emotionally. We also have confidence in the science because it's backed up by Scripture. So how do all these things correlate in a manner that will help us to overcome the trauma we face? The key is to control, or retrain, our mind by telling it the information we want it to show us and letting it capture the reality we see so it can dispel the negative it creates. By speaking truth, literally saying the words out loud or in our mind, we can begin to create a new neural pathway in our brain. We will quite literally rewire our brain to operate in a manner that is more productive.

It may seem uncomfortable at first, but most new things we try are uncomfortable until we get the hang of them. I think back

---

[12] Christopher Bergland, "Scientists Find That a Single Word Can Alter Percep-tions," *Psychology Today*, August 27, 2013. https://www.psychologytoday.com/us/blog/the-athletes-way/201308/scientists-find-single-word-can-alter-percep-tions.

to when I was first trying to learn drill. It was uncomfortable and foreign. It was difficult to change my body and mind to respond to unfamiliar commands in a precise, organized manner. However, over time and through repetition, I became proficient at it. Even today, I can still execute those drill commands at a moment's notice without much thought. It has become muscle memory.

Unpacking the Triggers

Take a moment to unpack some of those triggers that make you feel uncomfortable or cause you to panic. Some of you may know them right off the top of your head, while others may have no idea what causes you to have these thoughts and feelings. You may not know simply because you have never thought of it before. You may never have taken the time to sit down and investigate why you are having these thoughts and emotions. They just come upon you and overwhelm you.

Once you can identify your wrong thinking process, you can take steps to change your way of thinking. Your realization will be an aha moment that will lead to a lifetime of self-discovery, and you will be able to find the root cause of your mental wounds. Then, and only then, will you be able to overcome, because you will be able to treat the cause of your affliction and not just the symptoms. Take a few moments and write in your journal about the thoughts and emotions that have the most profound effect on your life—the ones that are stored in the emotional memory storehouse.

When my wife and I were first dating, we took a road trip to the Oregon coast. We left late in the afternoon, and since it was a six-hour drive, we knew we would be getting to our destination late in the evening. I drove the first part of the trip and swapped driving somewhere south of Salem. The plan was for her to drive until we reached Highway 38; then we would switch and I would drive. That section of highway has a treacherous mountain pass that has claimed the lives of many inexperienced drivers. With the late hour and unpredictable Oregon weather, I thought it would be best to take over driving for this part of the trip. While my wife—girlfriend at the time—drove her leg of the trip, I rested and fell asleep.

She woke me up, saying she needed to get gas and that it was my turn to drive. As she took the exit, I noticed that it was dark and there were no streetlights. I asked where we were, and she said she was taking the Highway 38 exit. In a moment, my brain put everything together. The fuel light was on, we were taking the mountain highway exit, and it was near midnight. These were three very bad things. You see, in Oregon you cannot pump your own gas, and in these small mountain towns everything closes early. So, there we were, miles from anywhere, and we were running on fumes.

I instantly began to fume myself. I freaked out. I began yelling and screaming about how she should have gotten gas earlier and that the gas stations were all closed. Not one of my better moments, I must admit. I was so mean that she got out of the car and started walking at midnight to the other side of the highway. To where, I don't know, and neither did she. She wasn't thinking that far ahead; she just knew she didn't feel safe in the car with me anymore, and her fight or flight kicked in. I was so angry I sped off back in the direction we had come to find an open gas station. Fortunately, I found one open about ten minutes away, but even more miraculous was that I convinced her to get back in the car with me. We both apologized and moved past this horrible experience—or so we thought.

From then on, every time she left the car near empty or the gas light would come on, I would have a similar reaction—not as extreme as before, but still not healthy. This reaction would in turn cause her to have anxiety about whether she left the car with enough gas in it. It was a constant battle in our marriage until one day she asked me why it was such a big deal to have the car full of gas all the time. I remember spouting off all the reasons: safety, responsibility, courtesy, etc. She asked again, "But why is it so important to you that it makes you have that kind of reaction?" I had to stop and think about it. Why did this cause such a visceral reaction? I had to identify what emotions, thoughts, and feelings I was having.

As I began to ponder this question, I unpacked my reaction to find out much more about myself and why my reaction was so severe. I realized that, for me, running out of gas was equivalent to a life-or-death situation. Why? Because in Iraq, if I ran out of gas, I could be in a life-or-death situation. Each time before I left a position, I filled up, checked the batteries, inventoried ammo, and accounted for water and maps. I was prepared. As I thought about Iraq and the consequences there, the feelings signaled danger about running out of gas, and the emotions were fear of death due to being unprepared.

This was my first of many aha moments. This was a mental wound I had covered up and not communicated about. So when I was triggered by my wife, I had a fight for survival overreaction. I had mental and physical wounds. I needed to unpack them. I had to allow myself and others into my head to identify the triggers that created the pain. I began to create a journal of similar reactions to benign situations and develop a function check to identify the true problem, not just the symptom of the problem. Once I could identify these things, it opened my mind to a whole host of other ideas.

What could I do about this newfound knowledge? Where else are my reactions based on wrong perceptions? How do I identify these areas and apply similar solutions?

Out of this experience and from years of fine-tuning, I created the mental function check.

Using the function check, journal about a time or an experience, or an emotion, thought, or feeling, that has caused you distress. Try to recall how your actions caused others around you distress. Write down with as much detail as possible your thoughts, feelings, and emotions. After a week, revisit these notes and begin to unpack these experiences using the function check. The function check is set up with a series of questions that will challenge your current way of thinking. Think of the function check as a candid interview with yourself.

Function Check:

- What sights, sounds, and memories are you experiencing?
- What do you see?
- What emotions or thoughts are attached?
- What do you hear?
- What emotions or thoughts are attached?
- What do you smell?
- What emotions or thoughts are attached?
- Mentally, where is your stress level?
- Do you recognize any triggers?
- Physically, how does your body feel?
- What sensations do you feel in your body?
- What emotions or thoughts are attached?
- Do you have any aches and pains?
- What emotions or thoughts are attached?
- Do you have any nausea, vomiting, or diarrhea?
- Spiritually, what is your heart condition?
- Are you experiencing grief or regret?
- What emotions or thoughts are attached?
- Are you experiencing depression?
- What emotions or thoughts are attached?
- How is your prayer life?
- Is God trying to show you something or release you from something?

Debrief

The subconscious mind is asking the questions, and it's the job of the rational conscious mind to find the answers. Once found, the conscious mind can now make better decisions based on this new intel. It's up to you to put these principles into action. You must do the work. I'll help you seek the appropriate intel, ammo, weapons, and support as you work with your memories, but you must design the conscious route for yourself and step off on patrol. You'll wage battles against yourself, your flesh, and your old way of thinking in the effort to unlearn the things that are causing you distress and become fully aware of the man God designed you to be. You must shake off the old man and become a new creation. Remember this key fact: You have a right to feel the way that you do, but that doesn't mean your feelings are always right.

CHAPTER 4

SOS:
STUCK ON STUPID

*There is nothing in this world man has created with his
hand that has not already been created in his mind.*
—Sgt Q

Personal Recon

WHEN I WAS IN GRAMMAR SCHOOL, I read about a study to increase
the free-throw percentages of the State University of New York's
basketball team. It was done in 1989 by Lori A. Ansbach at The

College of Brockport.[13] Until a few years ago, I didn't really grasp its importance.

While in school, I played a lot of basketball. I wasn't very good at it, but I was always looking for ways to improve. The study divided the team into two groups, A and B, and each recorded its free-throw percentage to get a baseline for the experiment. Group A practiced free throws a couple hours each day for two weeks. They recorded their starting numbers and ending numbers of free throws to see how much they would improve. Group B did the same. However, they didn't use a ball. Group B only went through the motions of shooting free throws, and instead they were instructed to imagine making every shot. I'm sure it was awkward at first shooting with an imaginary ball. Logic would tell you that when it came time to compare the numbers, the kids without the ball would show no improvement. But the results were stunning, and logic was wrong.

Group B's shot percentage improved more than Group A's! I remember thinking, *How strange that your imagination could make you better at free throws!* As expected, Group A's free throws also improved, so the researchers did a third group study with a Group C, and that group improved the most. Group C used the visualization technique along with physically shooting the ball. The combination of the two had the greatest percentage of improvement.

So what does this tell us? It tells us that our minds and thoughts will have a direct effect on the results in our lives. It also tells us that if we want superior results, we must not only imagine them in our minds, but we must take physical action to acquire them. We can't just dream, but we must take steps to create the reality of our dreams in the physical world.

This was the first time I realized our subconscious mind cannot

---

[13] Lori Ansbach Eckert, "The Effects of Mental Imagery on Free Throw Performance," *Kinesiology, Sport Studies, and Physical Education Master's Theses*, 3. *Digital Commons @Brockport*, https://digitalcommons.brockport.edu/pes_theses/3/.

SOS: STUCK ON STUPID

always tell the difference between what's real and what's imagined. When you really think about it, there's nothing in this world man creates with his hands that hasn't already been created in his mind.

How do we capitalize upon this? First, we must understand we're already doing it. We are already creating our reality in our minds and living out the result. The problem is that we're not always conscious of it, and thus we're probably creating problems for ourselves.

Let me explain. Have you ever had an argument with someone and stewed about it all day? How did that affect the rest of your day and the rest of your personal interactions with that person? When you replay a negative interaction, your mind finds similar information in its environment and brings it to your attention. It doesn't necessarily reason about it or provide a rational interpretation. It only presents information based on your current state of mind. It will continue to present similar negative interactions to show you the things you want or expect to see. These negative thoughts just keep building on each other.

I call this the SOS, or Stuck on Stupid, mode of our minds. In this chapter, I will show you a few studies that will expose this fatal flaw and explain how you can work to overcome it through a systematic process of engaging your rational, conscious mind and the truth to change the negative responses you normally experience.

Field Intel

"Negative bias is your brain's primal survival mechanism. It has allowed humanity to survive for thousands of years and to become the apex predator, dominating all other species on earth."[14]

I am going to take you a little deeper and show you how our minds can believe things that aren't happening. It gets strange from this point on, but stay with me; I'll bring it back around. As we begin to dissect some interesting studies, keep an open mind, and

[14] Hara E. Marano, "Our Brain's Negative Bias," *Psychology Today*, June 20, 2003, www.psychologytoday.com/us/articles/200306/our-brains-negative-bias.

I will show how the mind can trick the body and how we can use this knowledge to our advantage.

False pregnancy (pseudocyesis) is a condition where a woman, or even sometimes a man, believes they are pregnant and starts to develop physical signs of pregnancy when they aren't pregnant. The condition can last for weeks, months, and in rare cases, even years.

> When a woman feels an intense desire to get pregnant, which may be because of infertility, repeat miscarriages, impending menopause, or a desire to get married, her body may produce some pregnancy signs (such as a swollen belly, enlarged breasts, and even the sensation of fetal movement). The woman's brain then misinterprets those signals as pregnancy, and triggers the release of hormones (such as estrogen and prolactin) that lead to actual pregnancy symptoms.[15]

In other words, she is creating her own reality. Her thoughts are triggering emotions that are releasing chemicals that affect her brain regarding pregnancy. The want and desire flooding her take precedence over her rational mind, eventually causing the release of pregnancy hormones into her body and giving the physical sensation and appearance of a real pregnancy—even though no pregnancy has occurred. Fascinating.

Now that may be hard for some of us to accept or understand on a fundamental level because some of us are men and don't have a true reference regarding pregnancy. Everything we know is secondhand. Let's look at something we all know about, a term we're all familiar with to some degree—the placebo effect.

The placebo effect is a beneficial effect of a drug or substance that can't be attributed to the substance itself, so instead

[15] Traci C. Johnson, "False Pregnancy (Pseudocyesis): Causes, Symptoms, and Tests," *WebMD*, August 4, 2018, www.webmd.com/baby/false-pregnancy-pseudocyesis#1.

SOS: STUCK ON STUPID

is attributed to the belief in its power by the person who takes it. WebMD explains it like this:

> Research on the placebo effect has focused on the relationship of mind and body. One of the most common theories is that the placebo effect is due to a person's expectations. If a person expects a pill to do something, then it's possible that the body's own chemistry can cause effects similar to what a medication might have caused.[16]

This is another instance of how our mind and beliefs have great power over our body and our reality. The expectation of results can often produce results. We all know that what we practice, we get better at. I'm willing to bet we're all doing these things already. We're all using our minds to create our reality to some extent, though in many cases we may be doing it wrong. We surrender to the negative bias and subdue the mental anguish of our past. The negative bias will be covered extensively in the next chapter. For now, what you need to know is that the negative bias is your brain's primal survival mechanism. It has allowed humanity to survive for thousands of years and become the apex predator, dominating all other species on earth.

Now that you're familiar with the SOS concept, you can see that this is a person who is always negative, who lives their life from one calamity to the next. Every time you talk to them, they have some story about how they got screwed over or lost their job because someone was out to get them. Maybe they speak in absolutes: This *always* happens to me; I *never* get selected; my *entire* family hates me; my *whole* day was *filled* with problems.

Maybe this is something you do as well. I'm willing to bet we all do it from time to time, but remember, the more we practice

---

[16] Carol DerSarkissian, "The Placebo Effect: What Is It?" *WebMD*, February 08, 2018, www.webmd.com/pain-management/what-is-the-placebo-effect#1.

something, the better we get at it. This is simply "stuck on stupid." We're making our own reality. Allowing ourselves to get stuck on stupid and dwell on the negative aspects of the situation will in turn create more of the same problem we want to avoid. What we look for, we will find more of. In the later chapter "Change Your Thinking, Change Your Life," we will delve into this more and offer a great little experiment you can try that will accentuate this point.

Do our thoughts create our reality? Possibly at times, but they definitely can create how we perceive reality.

Let's use Sam as an example. Sam is a project coordinator for a large property development company. He has a big presentation to give at work, but wakes up a few minutes late, so he feels rushed and mumbles to himself about how stupid he is for pushing the snooze. He leaves for work without making his coffee because he's in a hurry, but he keeps thinking about how tired he is. When a guy cuts him off in traffic, he seethes: "What a jerk—he did that on purpose!" Then he sees that the gas needle is below E. He groans, thinking how dumb it was not to get gas yesterday. So now he's got to stop for gas when he's already feeling rushed.

We think, *We're never going to make it on time.* The attendant isn't as prompt as we'd like, so the next thought is, *That guy's a moron!* Just as we finish pumping the gas, a guy pulls in front of us blocking our way out. *This,* we think, *always happens to me!* Now the world is out to get us.

Once you get to the office, you find there's no coffee made. *What's wrong with Sally? She can't even make coffee like she's supposed to. She never gets anything right.* You finally make it to the meeting and give the presentation to the team, but wouldn't you know it—they decide to use another proposal for the project. *Nobody ever chooses my ideas! They must not like me.* You spend the rest of the morning worrying about being fired because they didn't choose your project proposal. *How am I going to pay my bills? My rent?*

At lunch, you feel depressed, so you choose not to join the other team members for lunch. *Hey, they didn't invite me anyway.*

They all think they're better than I am. In the afternoon, you get distracted and forget to submit your daily report, which your boss reminds you about as you leave for the day. You think, *I'm always in trouble; it's like my boss just waits for me to mess something up so he can yell at me.*

You drive home even more depressed and tell your wife about the horrible day you had, recalling how these things *always* happen to you and how you can *never* catch a break. You begin to stew on the day's events, and soon the worry turns to anxiety as thoughts of getting fired begin to manifest. All the evidence is there: You believe your coworkers don't like you, your boss hates you, and no one likes your project ideas. You feel as though everything always turns out poorly for you.

Maybe all of this doesn't apply to you, but I'm willing to bet that a good portion of it does. I know I've gone down these SOS rabbit holes far more than I'd like to admit. According to the Nobel Prize-winning scientist Daniel Kahneman, the average person has 20,000 interactions or moments with people in a given day.[17] Twenty thousand! That's a lot. How much time would it take you to make 20,000 dollars, or make 20,000 cookies, or shoot 20,000 free throws? Could you do any of those in a single day? Maybe, but it would be tough. Yet having 20,000 interactions seems effortless.

Sam's story is about absolutes. *Always* and *never* are absolutes. If we go back and unpack the story, we can start to see the lies. Did you notice that partway through the story the subject changed from *Sam* to *we* to *you*? I'm betting you didn't catch it, and if you did, you dismissed it without much thought. That's how easy it is to ignore the things right in front of us. These subtle changes happen in our minds as the negative bias begins to steer our day.

Let's analyze one of Sam's interactions. The guy cutting Sam off was negative, but was it because Sam wasn't paying attention to traffic? Was he still thinking about how he forgot about the presen-

---

[17] https://news.gallup.com/businessjournal/12916/big-impact-small-interactions.aspx.

tation and pressed the snooze button? Was it because he was feeling rushed? Was he driving slowly because he was looking for a gas station, and the other driver got tired of waiting for him to turn? This perceived negative interaction compounded an already stress-filled morning that harbored further negative self-talk and continued to affect every other interaction that Sam had that day.

When Sam gets home, he recaps his day to his wife and tells her how bad his day was. He only recaps six or seven interactions he had that day, whereas Sam had 19,993 other interactions that were not negative at all. Due to our negative bias, we tend to focus on the few negative interactions and dismiss everything else. We must learn or retrain ourselves to counteract this bias by pointing out to ourselves the positive interactions we have or the things we're grateful for. Positive psychology expert John Gottman suggests that it takes five positive interactions to counteract one negative interaction.[18] That's a five-to-one ratio. This further underscores our need to be vigilant with our thoughts if we plan on overcoming our negative bias and prevent becoming stuck on stupid.

Scripture Unpack

All change must first be born in our mind and incubated
in our hearts before it can be birthed into our lives.
—Sgt Q

"As a dog returns to his own vomit, so a fool repeats his folly" (Proverbs 26:11 NKJV). Wow! What a descriptive verse to show how people will continue to return to the very things that caused them pain, discomfort, and sickness! I've heard many pastors use this verse to speak about sin, sexual immorality, drunkenness, and addiction—all good examples that we can apply this verse to. Now I'm going to show you how we can apply the Bible to all areas of

---

[18] Benson, Kyle, "The Magic Relationship Ratio, According to Science," *The Gottman Institute*, October 4, 2017, www.gottman.com/blog/the-magic-relationship-ratio-according-science/.

our lives, not just the areas others can see. But first, we have to understand what sin is. Sin is the condition of fallen humanity before Christ redeems us through faith in Him and the rebirth He gives. It permeates and affects every aspect of our nature.

It's easy for people to see your sin when they're looking for it, but what if your sin is in your thoughts? It's much harder for others to see that sin, and if they do, they can't recognize it for what it is. They can only see the *symptoms* of your thoughts played out in the behavior you exhibit because of your wrong, or sinful, way of thinking.

Your sinful, wrong thoughts affect you more than anyone else. They will cause anxiety and panic if left unchecked. Our negative, sinful thought life will cause us to damage relationships and be isolated from loved ones because we'll continue to look for the negative. We'll continue to pick apart every interaction until we find something negative to focus on. Jesus warns us that our sin is not just outward behavior, but inward thoughts as well. In the gospel of Matthew, He gives us two examples:

> You have heard that it was said to those of old, "You shall not murder; and whoever murders will be liable to judgment." But I say to you that everyone who is angry with his brother will be liable to judgment; whoever insults his brother will be liable to the council; and whoever says, "You fool!" will be liable to the hell of fire. (Matthew 5:21–22 ESV)

> You have heard that it was said, "You shall not commit adultery." But I say to you that everyone who looks at a woman with lustful intent has already committed adultery with her in his heart. (Matthew 5:27–28 ESV)

In both examples, Jesus tells us that not only our behavior, but also our thoughts can be counted as sin. James, the half-brother of Jesus, expounds on this teaching by saying it is not the thought that produces sin; rather, it is the *submission* or surrender to the thought that is the birth of sin. Before Christ enters our lives, we are slaves to sin and have no power to save ourselves from it or to change ourselves. "But each person is tempted when he is lured and enticed by his own desire. Then desire when it has conceived gives birth to sin, and sin when it is fully grown brings forth death" (James 1:14–15 ESV).

Therefore, do not surrender to the fleeting thoughts you have, but control your thoughts by using your conscious mind to subdue them and to regulate the ones you're having. Let me be clear: fleeting thoughts and emotions are not the problem here, but dwelling on and yielding to destructive fantasy, or reliving destructive past events, is the problem.

Knowing what Jesus and James said about our thought life, we can look closer at Proverbs 26:11 (NKJV): "As a dog returns to his own vomit, so a fool repeats his folly." When we dwell on a negative experience, such as getting cut off in traffic, and surrender to it, it can fester and grow into sin in our life that begins to control us. Whether we realize it or not, sinful or negative thoughts, if left unchecked, will lead to their manifestation in action. Some people will call this a self-fulfilling prophecy, but in actuality it's our sinful nature born in our thoughts and hearts that becomes reality. Jesus shows us this progression in Matthew 15:18–19 (ESV): "But what comes out of the mouth proceeds from the heart, and this defiles a person. For out of the heart come evil thoughts, murder, adultery, sexual immorality, theft, false witness, slander."

Our sin can appear as a negative thought that, once it takes root, develops into evil and eventually grows beyond our thoughts to manifest in our actions. If we want to change a behavior we can see, we must first change our hearts. To do this, we must first repent and ask Christ for the power of the Holy Spirit to help us change the way we are thinking about people and situations. All change must first be born in our mind and incubate in our heart before it can be birthed into our life and action. This is the natural way of things in the world. Think of any invention or gadget that has ever been created. It first must have been conceived as a thought, then incubated in the heart before it was created.

When we look at the extreme end of how our negative thoughts create grim realities, we need look no further than the serial killers in our society. A quick study of the most prolific serial killers ascertains a common thread that runs through them all. All their crimes started out as fleeting thoughts in their minds. Interviews with these serial killers reveal that they all reported that their crimes started in their minds, where they played them out, rehearsing them over and over until they could no longer control them. "Eventually, however, the fantasy is not enough to fulfill the need. Thus, when serial killers mature from their remote fantasies, their fantasies become a cognitive staging ground for actual crimes"[19]

At what point could they have stopped? That must differ with each person, but the point is that thoughts left unchecked can give way to fantasy. These fantasies manifest in compulsive behavior that eventually becomes reality in the form of murder. The serial killers entertained their fantasies until they were overwhelmed by them to the point where lawlessness and rebellion ruled them and they violated the social structure of our society and murdered innocent people.[20]

God says there is a point where He gives people over to their degraded nature (Romans 1:28) because they delight in wickedness (2 Thessalonians 2:12). That's a very important reason to control our thoughts and turn to Christ for help.

We can see how King David took this same pathway as he witnessed Bathsheba bathing on the rooftop. We can understand he must have watched her and created a fantasy about her in his

[19] Meher Sharma, "The Development of Serial Killers: A Grounded Theory Study," Masters Theses. 3720, (Eastern Illinois University, 2018), https://the-keep.eiu.edu/theses/3720. This URL provides a download link for the entire paper.
[20] Meher Sharma, "The Development of Serial Killers"

mind—a fantasy that quickly became reality when he allowed himself to surrender to his impure thoughts and take her as a lover. He recognized his sin, but instead of turning from it, he indulged his desire to escape accountability, and then committed murder to cover his indiscretion. Both examples show that when we indulge these negative, sinful thoughts, they can, and often do, manifest as a terrible presence. These examples are on opposite ends of the spectrum when it comes to heroes and villains, which further underscores the fact that no one is immune to the temptation of giving ourselves over to our negative thought life and evil fantasies.

The Bible calls King David a man after God's own heart (1 Samuel 13:14; Acts 13:22). Yet David—an anointed man of God who walked closely with God, a man who had been delivered many times by the hand of God—still could not overcome the progression of his own thoughts manifesting from temptation into a murderous reality.

We can learn two very important things from this example. First, no one is immune to yielding to negative or sinful thinking. Heroes and villains alike—both at bottom have the same ability to manifest their thought lives into reality. We must learn how to control this mental ability and use it to choose life and not death.

Second, at any point we can turn our sinful thoughts around before they become truth. We can repent as David did and leave those things at the altar. We can change our thought life and begin to create a new life from the ashes of our past. We can hold on to the hope as David did and allow God to heal the wounds we have created. We can surrender ourselves to God and fight diligently against the negative bias, the negative thoughts and compulsions, the sinful patterns that bombard us daily. The more we resist these temptations and flee from the negative thought patterns, the stronger we will become at resisting them. For those who belong to Christ, the power of the Holy Spirit is always available for overcoming.

When we have those negative thoughts, we must dispatch them quickly with truth, positive affirmation, and prayer. We are still at war; we are on the battlefield of the mind. I will show you how to repurpose the battle tactics you already know through practice and diligence to claim victory over the effects of war and the thoughts that would seek to control you. Do not let your mind return to its old way of thinking.

Tactical Application

Everything isn't perfect every day, but it's a waste of time
and energy dwelling on the negative.
—Sgt Q

We are prewired to focus on the negative, to yield to sin. In one sense, this destructive predisposition to negative experience can serve as a safeguard to increase our survival rate. It has been essential in keeping humanity alive. However, if left unchecked, it can cause us a myriad of other problems, like it did with Sam, the project coordinator who hit the snooze button. Let's delve into our own lives and find our own negative bias, our destructive sinful patterns. The Bible says to examine ourselves and make sure we are in the faith (that is, standing on the truth of the Bible; see 2 Corinthians 13:5). So now that you are aware, let's practice.

Unpack the patterns in your life. Think of one negative interaction you had in the last seventy-two hours, and thoroughly examine it. Pick it apart and see what you find. Did you spend an incredible amount of time ruminating on that interaction? Did your brain pull memories from the file of similar events and past hurts? Have you replayed it in your head over and over? Is your rehearsing of the negative event making it even stronger? Have you thought of all the things you wish you would have said and done?

Okay, now let's combat those with positive experiences or positive outcomes. You are looking to establish that five-to-one ratio, so you need five other facts to present to your mind. Not only do you need to think of them, but you also need to frame them to yourself correctly as well. Let's use Sam's experience of getting cut off in traffic as our example. This instance gets to me personally. I find myself having to remember these five things on a regular basis.

Negative experience: Getting cut off in traffic.

Reframed thoughts and emotions:

1. I'm safe.
2. I'm grateful I have a car I can drive.
3. I'm thankful that the A/C is running strong.
4. I sure do enjoy this comfortable seat.
5. I'm thankful I have a job to drive to.

But above all, I'm grateful that God has promised to watch over me and be with me at all times. His angels surround me. I can turn to His Word and promises and the power of His Holy Spirit to help me. Psalm 91 is a good example.

Now you try. Use the example you wrote down earlier. Create five positive points you can tell yourself that will reframe that experience. Be specific and deliberate in the words you use.

Negative experience:

Reframed thoughts and emotions:

1. I'm...
2.
3.
4.
5.

It is also just as important to frame them in the correct manner. You wouldn't say, "Don't look down" to someone afraid of heights as they're crossing a bridge. That action would be detrimental as it would automatically entice them to look down. It's important to frame our thoughts correctly. Here are some poorly framed examples regarding Sam's experience:

1. I'm glad he didn't hit my car.
2. I hope he isn't going to the same place I am.
3. Where's a cop? This guy needs a ticket.
4. I hope he doesn't hit someone else.
5. I hope he gets what's coming to him.

These are much easier things to say in the moment when our emotions are running high. So take great care when forming your thoughts and when you notice yourself getting SOS. Stop and reassess your thoughts and see how your outlook changes. Look at your reframed thoughts about your experience. Did you frame your positive truth-talk correctly? If not, then take some time to correct it now.

This, like any new skill, takes time and patience to master. Once you start this process, you will begin to diligently practice approaching each interaction with a positive appreciation. You won't have to fake it. Everything isn't perfect every day, but it's a waste of time and energy dwelling on the negative. Among your 20,000 interactions on any given day, I'm confident you can find some positive aspects to focus on.

Now turn to the Bible and ask the Holy Spirit to help you find at least three verses that fit your situation. There are many tools to help you do this if you are unfamiliar with the Bible or have never used it in this way before. There are many Bible apps available for free, as well as using Google to find Bible verses and using one of the many websites that give expositions of the chosen verse. A common practice for me is to put the verse in the search bar, then add "Gill explains or exposition" after the verse. Pastor John Gill was a Baptist theologian in the 1700s at the same church that Charles Spurgeon later pastored. I like to read Gill's writings because they are very practical, and he doesn't have an agenda to write what is culturally popular as we might find in some Christian books today.

However, the best place to seek guidance is from a pastor in your local church. Not all churches are created equal, so you will have to find one that fits well with your season of life. My only advice on selecting a church is to make sure they are preaching directly from the Bible. Test the pastor by taking notes and looking up the Scriptures on your own to ensure he is true to the context of the part of the Bible he is teaching from. You can also request to look at the church's statement of faith, values, and vision to make sure they are a Bible-teaching church. Once you find a pastor, church leadership, and community you trust, ask for help in applying Scripture to your situation.

Your success depends on your ability to use the tools you are given. It never fails that several months after I take a team of veterans through Operation Restore Hope, a veteran approaches me who is still struggling mightily. They will tell me of all the things going wrong and how things were great in the beginning, but now they are back to square one. They claim the program didn't work. Upon further investigation, it quickly becomes apparent they were not using the tools they were given, and subsequently the lack of tools led to failure. These weapons only work if you wield them properly.

I once watched a video of a young private on the firing range. He was in prone position, aiming downrange and engaging targets. However, he was very dismayed that he suddenly stopped scoring hits no matter what adjustments he made, whereas a few minutes prior he was scoring good hits and tracking center mass. The men pulling the targets were not even registering hits on the paper at all. Frustrated, the private called one of the PMIs (Personal Marksman Instructors) over to help assess the situation. He explained what was happening and that there must be some malfunction with the weapon, that it's useless, and he needs a new one. The PMI looked over the weapon and without touching it, only through observation, realized the cause of the problem. He yelled and half laughed at the private, "You have no more ammo, private!" The magazine had run dry, and the private had fired all the ammo and never reloaded. Even though he had additional ammo, he wasn't using it. Instead, he blamed the weapon for malfunctioning when it was working just as it had been designed to. This problem was what we referred to in the military as OE, or Operator Error. As you move forward with this process, make sure you're using your weapons properly and that they're filled with ammo so you can hit the center on all your targets.

Debrief

For those of us dealing with posttraumatic stress, the need to overcome our negative bias is even more important. If we don't correct this negative thought pattern, it will quickly spiral into anxiety or a full-blown panic attack, and none of us want that. We know we have a negative bias. We know our negative and sinful thought patterns will cause us to find more and more negative interactions. What we focus on, we will find more of.

Have you ever had a negative interaction with someone, then spent hours contemplating what you would say or do when you saw them again? Or have you played it over and over again? As we do this, more and more "bad" things happen, and it seems like everything is rotten. Traffic was bad. Your lunch order was wrong. Then your wife is on your case because you didn't mow the lawn. I propose that the day is not good or bad; it's that our intentions for the day, our attitudes, are good or bad. By consistently looking for the good in your day, you will create a heart of gratitude and be surprised how your attitude and outlook will improve along with your social interactions. A therapist I once used told me, "Don't let someone live in your head rent free." Think about that for a moment.

Doing the exercises in this book have helped me change my perceptions, and the same practice can help you as well. With practice, these exercises will build on one another and develop into a personal battle plan for you to use in your daily life. These same exercises have proven very successful for many others who have gone through our program, Operation Restore Hope.

CHAPTER 5

NEGATIVE BIAS:

OUR SURVIVAL MECHANISM AND HOW IT CONDITIONS OUR MINDS

Negative bias is our mind putting more significance on painful or negative memories so we can avoid making the same mistake time and time again.
—Sgt Q

Personal Recon

WHEN I WAS MAYBE TEN YEARS old, some of my friends and I got into the liquor cabinet at the house of one of their aunts. I grabbed a bottle of Black Velvet, a whiskey that was first barreled in 1951 with the original name of Black Label. The name quickly changed after the original distiller, Jack Napier, sampled the first batch and commented on its uncommon velvety taste and smoothness.[21] The ads sounded great: crystal-clear Canadian water . . . finest ingredients.

I knew none of this as we snuck off to the backyard to drink it. Having never experienced alcohol before, we drank the whole bottle very quickly. The effect hit me with tremendous speed. At first I was all laughter and euphoria, but then it quickly turned to regret as the earth began to spin out of control. I can still remember clutching the lawn in the backyard for fear of flying out of the earth's gravitational pull and into the dark void of space. My stomach was in a continual state of feeling like a somersault, resulting in the immediate expulsion of the poison I'd consumed thirty minutes earlier. The retching continued for hours, and as the day progressed, I felt like death warmed over. It wasn't until the next morning that I reached the tail end of my misery.

To this day, I can't stand the smell of Black Velvet. Even a whiff of it sends my stomach into an involuntary fit of knots, warning me of the danger of the substance. Though I'm now a responsible adult and could easily reason that, in moderation, a glass of Black Velvet would not render the same result, my subconscious mind remembers my ten-year-old self and the trauma my body experienced that day. It fires off all sorts of warning shots to me about Black Velvet in an effort to save me from the harm I once experienced. Ladies and gentlemen, this is what psychologists call the negative bias, or operant conditioning, in which our brain puts more significance on painful or negative memories so we can avoid making the same mistake time and time again. The concept of negative bias describes a useful survival mechanism that helps us avoid danger.

---

[21] "Our Heritage," *Black Velvet*, http://www.blackvelvetwhisky.com/heritage.

Field Intel

If left unchecked, [negativity bias] will lead us down a
dark and terror-filled path, even if only in our mind.
—Sgt Q

An article by Hara Marano discusses a study conducted by Ohio State University psychologist John Cacioppo, who explains why he believes negative comments stick with us longer than positive ones. Marano says that Cacioppo believes that this is:

> Due to the brain's "negativity bias": your brain is simply built with a greater sensitivity to unpleasant news. The bias is so automatic that it can be detected at the earliest stage of the brain's information processing. . . . Cacioppo showed people pictures known to arouse positive feelings (such as a Ferrari or a pizza), those certain to stir up negative feelings (like a mutilated face or dead cat), and those known to produce neutral feelings (a plate, a hair dryer).[22]

While showing these pictures, the patients were having the electrical activity in their brains' cerebral cortexes monitored to learn the "magnitude of information processing taking place"[23] with all three types of pictures. Marano explains that Cacioppo showed that:

> The brain reacts more strongly to stimuli it deems negative. [Negative images created] a greater surge in

---

[22] Hara Estroff Marano, "Why We Love Bad News," *Psychology Today*, May 27, 2003, https://www.psychologytoday.com/us/articles/200305/why-we-love-bad-news.

[23] Marano, "Why We Love Bad News."

electrical activity. Thus, our attitudes are more heavily influenced by downbeat news than good news.

Our capacity to weigh negative input so heavily evolved for a good reason—to keep us out of harm's way. From the dawn of human history our very survival depended on our skill at dodging danger. The brain developed systems that would make it unavoidable for us not to notice danger and thus, hopefully, respond to it.[24]

As I began to study my brain and how it operates, I became aware of many remarkable studies in the fields of human psychology and the functionality of the brain. I have included some of them in this book for you. All references can be found in the endnotes, and I encourage you to read the entire studies. They are fascinating, and I'm sure you'll glean bits of knowledge from them that I couldn't fit into this book.

There is another incredible condition that illustrates how the negative bias can work, even for a perceived future event: Retired Husband Syndrome. Yes, it's a real thing.

Retired Husband Syndrome (RHS) is a psychosomatic, stress-related illness that has been estimated to occur in 60 percent of Japan's elder female population. It's a condition where a woman begins to exhibit signs of physical illness and depression as her husband reaches, or approaches, retirement. This is due to the fact that most Japanese men work away from home for long periods of time, returning for only short stints of time during their careers. Thus, the running of the household and daily affairs are left to the wives.[25]

Japan is a very male-dominated society with not much value

[24] Marano, "Why We Love Bad News."

[25] Anthony Faiola, "Sick of Their Husbands in Graying Japan," *Washington Post*, October 17, 2005, https://www.washingtonpost.com/wp-dyn/content/article/2005/10/16/AR2005101601145.html.

given to a woman's opinion or needs. With the impending retirement on the horizon, the wife grows more anxious, knowing her control of her affairs and home will be unsettled when her husband begins staying at home and will likely assume control of her daily activities. In these cases, the wife is under the thumb of the husband. Prior to retirement, the husband is only home for short amounts of time, which for the wife is bearable, but with the looming retirement of her husband on the horizon, those negative past interactions of her husband being at home begin to manifest as anxiety and depression as she contemplates her inevitable future. The mind is recalling those negative experiences and focusing on them for self-preservation. Although positive experiences may outweigh the negative ones, the mind uses negative bias to focus on the negative.

One outcome related to RHS is divorce. A study in 2004 showed that Japan has seen its divorce rate quadruple since 1985. It projected that the numbers would rise even further by 2006 as the baby-boomer generation enters retirement. This study by Marco Bertoni and Giorgio Brunello of the University of Padova cites RHS as being a major contributing factor in divorce.[26]

> Some women deal with RHS by focusing their energy on obsessions such as collecting teddy bears, or following a celebrity, which they say can help them psychologically. They may also ask their husbands to stay on at work past retirement age. Many wives do not tell their husbands what is happening and this can worsen the stress as their husbands may not understand or even realize their wives are RHS sufferers.[27]

---

[26] Marco Bertoni and Giorgio Brunello, "Pappa Ante Portas: The Retired Husband Syndrome in Japan," IZA DP No. 8350 (IZA, July 2014), http://ftp.iza.org/dp8350.pdf

[27] "Retired Husband Syndrome," Revolvy, https://www.revolvy.com/page/Retired-husband-syndrome?cr=1, accessed January 30, 2020.

Negative bias, if left unchecked, will lead anyone down a dark and terror-filled path, even if only in their minds.

This mechanism is attached to our deep-seated emotions and overrides all logic and reasoning. Since we are all logical, reasoning beings, we must make reason our primary decision-making avenue. In today's modern society, we have less need for the negative bias in a physical sense because danger is not lurking around every corner, and most animals in our daily environment are not hunting us for food.

We also need this part of the brain less because we are lectured and taught from previous generations about dangers in our environment. We are bombarded with safety tips and strategies, almost to the point of being overwhelmed with information. So we as a species have become very good at eliminating danger from our path.

We learn of dangers in our environment at a young age from things like warning labels on our toys and food containers. Case in point: a plastic bag has a warning label on it that says, "Do not put your head in the bag as it can cause suffocation." Some of you think this is ridiculous. Everyone should know that, so why do we need to label the bag? Well, it's because someone at some point did put the bag over their head, and they died. As logical and reasoning beings, we decide that we needed to warn others of this danger so they wouldn't meet the same fate. You see, those who knew the person who suffocated in the bag would have a strong negative bias to putting their head in a plastic bag, but those who did not know the story firsthand would not have the same negative bias associated with plastic bags, and they may attempt the same experience, unaware of the consequences.

Take a moment to think of all the warnings on all the products in our lives. It's probably easier to list the things that don't have warning labels than those that do. I know some of you are on the fence right now. It's okay. These are new concepts you've always experienced, but may never have thought about in this way. Right now, you're trying to reconcile what you're reading with the life experiences you've had. If you were on the fence before, you won't be after this next section. I'm going to blow the doors wide open on how advertisers and politicians use this negative bias to control what we think, control what we buy, and control how we vote.

Why do we have warning labels on cigarettes? Everyone knows they cause cancer. Well, just because people know something does not mean they trust it. Cigarettes have had written warnings on them for years, but research has shown that using graphic images of the consequences of smoking reduces the number of smokers more. In 2016, a study by researchers at the Penn Tobacco Center of Regulatory Science (TCORS) at the Annenberg School for Communication found that warning labels featuring photos of real smokers who were harmed by their habit were more effective at getting smokers to quit than the text-only labels currently in use."[28]

Using real people and real stories changed dangerous behaviors. Interesting. People know smoking is dangerous, but they do not see the effects until much later in life when it's already too late to reverse the damage. The negative bias never gets activated for this behavior. However, when we can see descriptive images of real people suffering from the effects of smoking, it triggers the survival mechanism, and smoking rates fall. *Science Daily* published a report on another study that sought to support this research:

> "Potential Effectiveness of Pictorial Warning Labels That Feature the Images and Personal Details of Real People," which will be published in *Nicotine & Tobacco Research,* tested images that graphically showed real people harmed by smoking—an appeal that is both factual and emotional.
>
> Our aim in this study was to find out how smokers

[28] University of Pennsylvania, "Study Shows Effectiveness of Testimonial Warning Labels on Tobacco Products," *Medical Xpress—Medical Research Advances and Health News,* December 12, 2016, https://medicalxpress.com/news/2016-12-effectiveness-testimonial-tobacco-products.html.

respond to cigarette pack warning labels that use photo-
graphs of real people whose health has been affected by
their own, or by someone else's, smoking.[29]

During the study, adult smokers viewed several labels from one
of three categories:

- Labels that showed a photograph of a real person who had
  been harmed by smoking, some of which were accompa-
  nied by a short text description of the person
- The FDA's previous image-based warning labels
- The text-only warning labels currently in use in the United
  States

Participants were then asked to report their initial response to
the labels and their intentions to quit smoking. Five weeks later, the
researchers followed up to see if the smokers had made any attempts
to quit, and if so, how successful they had been. They found that
warning labels containing images consistently outperformed text-
only labels. Among the smokers who viewed the text-only labels,
7.4 percent of smokers attempted to quit in the subsequent five
weeks. Those who viewed the testimonial photos from real smokers, however, had a quit attempt rate of 15.4 percent—roughly
double—and were four times as likely to be successful. "There's a
stickiness to the testimonial photos—the suffering of real people in
real contexts—and they increased the likelihood that people would
attempt to quit and stay quit," says senior author Joseph N. Cappella, PhD Gerald R. Miller, Professor of Communication at the
Annenberg School, suggested that people are more engaged with
facts when those facts are imbued with the emotions of real life.
When smokers could see the actual effects of their behavior, the

---

[29] "Study Shows Effectiveness of Testimonial Warning Labels on Tobacco
Products," *ScienceDaily*, December 12, 2016, www.sciencedaily.com/
releases/2016/12/161212105317.htm.

negative bias was activated, making a strong emotional connection with their current behavior. This led many of them to quit.[30]

Now consider the news—the political rhetoric advertising. How many of these things are targeting your negative bias in an attempt to change your behavior? Just this morning, I saw a video on social media about a family hit by a drunk driver, killing their two little girls. They retold the story in graphic detail. A child died, and the mother was found cradling the decapitated head of the child when the paramedics arrived. I can guarantee with certainty that those who witnessed this tragedy, the first responders and the friends and family, will have an enormous negative bias regarding drinking and driving. I am confident those directly impacted by this real-life event will not drink and drive. The negative bias will override behavior. The family said they chose to share their story in graphic detail because they wanted others to think twice about getting behind the wheel while intoxicated. Knowingly or unknowingly, they are attempting to engage the brain's negative bias to alter behavior.

Knowledge is power, and now that you know of this survival mechanism, you'll be able to see the world in a new way. You'll be able to discern when the media or a politician is attempting to use this part of your brain to override behavior. The message may be good. It may be relevant, and behavior change could be beneficial. But you have the power to logically deduce for yourself the best solution and not allow your primitive brain to choose for you. We are all logical, thinking beings, so don't be controlled by your subconscious emotions.

Okay, now that we're all on the same page and have the same understanding of negative bias, we can start to unpack some of the trauma in our lives and see where this negative bias is causing

---

[30] Emily Brennan, Erin Maloney, Yotam Ophir, Joseph N. Cappella, "Potential Effectiveness of Pictorial Warning Labels That Feature the Images and Personal Details of Real People," *Nicotine & Tobacco Research* (2016), DOI: 10.1093/ntr/ntw319.

friction. To truly find these things and overcome them, we must work backward from symptom to cause. When we have an anger outburst or become excessively emotional from a seemingly normal instance, we need to pay close attention and ask ourselves, Why is this causing me such distress?

Our emotional brain often overrides logic in these moments, so we have a reaction that damages relationships. We do learn something from them, though. We learn to avoid those things, people, or situations that make us uncomfortable. The negative bias will correlate a person or situation with danger and will therefore avoid it at all costs. When we find ourselves around a similar situation, our body will have a visceral reaction as the amygdala hijack is initiated. We will cover this in more depth in another chapter, but for now, just know that the negative bias, if left unchecked, will cause us to have emotional outbursts and panic attacks and will isolate us from society.

What things are we avoiding because of our negative bias?

Scripture Unpack

Reframed thoughts will become your weapon to fight the darkness in your mind.

How can we use this knowledge to overcome posttraumatic stress? How do we learn to control our reality? Proverbs 23:7 (NKJV) says, "For as he thinks in his heart, so is he. 'Eat and drink!' he says to you, but his heart is not with you."

"For as he thinks in his heart, so is he." The warning here is that a ruler is allowing you to feast at his table, not for your own gain, but for his. His motives are not pure. God sees not only our actions, but our motives as well. He wants us to change our hearts and our minds, and only He can help us do that. To change our minds, we must change the way we think; we must change the conversation in our head. But we must have *changed hearts* in order to really do that. We began to explore our thought life and how God views it in the SOS chapter. Now we're going to go a bit deeper into the abyss and look at how our brains and minds function.

What thoughts are you allowing to come into your head?

What memories are you entertaining?

As we looked at the placebo effect, we saw that it showed that our thoughts can create a chemical reaction in our bodies that mimic the results of medication based upon our own expectations. That's amazing! What does the Bible say about this phenomenon? Romans 12:2 (ESV) says, "Do not be conformed to this world, but be transformed by the renewal of your mind, that by testing you may discern what is the will of God, what is good and acceptable and perfect."

Again, be transformed by the renewing of your mind. Set your mind on the things of God and not of this world. That is a powerful concept to follow, and it's even more difficult to allow yourself to trust that He will lead you on a path of godly living instead of following your own path.

God can use our weaknesses for His glory, but we must be willing to share them. God called me to lead this mission of helping other veterans heal from the effects of war, just as He helped heal me. However, I wanted nothing to do with it. I had already created a successful start-up company with over eighty employees. No way did I want to put that on the back burner and start over again. It was far too much work! Not to mention that I always felt that my combat experience was not stellar enough to constitute leading other combat veterans toward healing.

Yes, I had been in a high-speed unit—I was a close combat instructor, a master parachutist, and more. Regardless, my actual trigger time was minor in comparison to that of many others. I was perfectly content with knowing others had it worse and that someone more qualified should be leading this mission. My experience paled in comparison to that of my comrades. This held me back more than anything. It wasn't until God showed me how to reframe those negative thoughts that I understood how to function with this level of healing. He told me that others had more combat experience than me, but even with my limited combat experience, my struggles were real, the nightmares were real, the panic attacks were real, and the audio hallucinations were also real. God helped me realize that if I was struggling with those things in my limited experience, how much more were the other veterans struggling from their extensive combat record.

There you have it. God reframed my negative thoughts and turned them toward empowerment. God showed me how to overcome the negative bias. I also learned God was giving me a second chance to help my brothers, even though I felt I hadn't done enough for them when I was in Iraq. This reframed thought became my weapon against the hurt and the feeling of inadequacy holding me back. The same can be true for you. You don't have to be labeled as a victim of posttraumatic stress, but you can be transformed with new thoughts and beliefs based on truth from God. These will become your weapon to fight the darkness in your mind. You can learn to speak truth over your pain and repeat it every time memories arise. What the enemy tried to use for evil, God can use for good. Through your trial, through your pain, you, too, can bring strength and healing to others. But first, for those of you reading this who may not be Christians, let's look at exactly how God accomplishes it.

It's important to understand that we can't experience deep and lasting change and walk in the Holy Spirit without belonging to Jesus Christ. What does that mean? The Bible teaches in Ephesians 2:1–5 (NKJV) that all people are dead in their sins, follow the ways of the world instead of God's ways, and live under the devil's reign until they trust in Christ:

> And you He made alive, who were dead in trespasses and sins, in which you once walked according to the course of this world, according to the prince of the power of the air, the spirit who now works in the sons of

disobedience, among whom also we all once conducted ourselves in the lusts of our flesh, fulfilling the desires of the flesh and of the mind, and were by nature children of wrath, just as the others.

But God, who is rich in mercy, because of His great love with which He loved us, even when we were dead in trespasses, made us alive together with Christ (by grace you have been saved).

The solution is what the apostle Peter says: "Repent, and let every one of you be baptized in the name of Jesus Christ for the remission of sins; and you shall receive the gift of the Holy Spirit" (Acts 2:38 NKJV). Repent means to turn around. Jesus says we must be *born again* (John 3:3).

This initial yielding to God in Christ is called justification, which means being declared innocent before God even though we are sinners. Once this takes place, the Holy Spirit begins to grow us in Christ, renewing the whole man through the transformation of our spirit, soul, and body (the brain being part of the body). This process is called sanctification, or growing in holiness, and it takes the rest of our lives. But trying to walk in the Holy Spirit without first being justified just can't work (Romans 12:1–2).

The Holy Spirit is working through QMissions mainly in the area of sanctification and doing good works by the power of the Holy Spirit, and part of those good works involves the renewing of our minds. Galatians 5:13 (NKJV) says, "For you, brethren, have been called to liberty; only do not use liberty as an opportunity for the flesh [that is, the fallen mind], but through love serve one another."

Being renewed by the Holy Spirit is not just a matter of positive self-talk, unlike what's called prosperity teaching (we've all seen the teachers telling us we can make a million dollars) or cognitive behavioral therapy, though there may be some limited help there. Positive self-talk will not free us from sin and evil. Instead, it's a matter of truth. Just telling yourself you're getting better and better will not stand the test of reality. You need the power of God found in His Word. Furthermore, we have to avoid getting caught up in shallow and empty ideas and viewpoints that only go skin-deep. Paul warns about these in Colossians 2:8–10 (NKJV):

> Beware lest anyone cheat you through philosophy and empty deceit, according to the tradition of men, according to the basic principles of the world, and not according to Christ. For in Him dwells all the fullness of the Godhead bodily; and you are complete in Him, who is the head of all principality and power.

As we look at these psychological techniques and concepts, while they can be helpful, our primary purpose is to be renewed by the Holy Spirit in our minds, and He does that through the Word of God. It's important not to be double-minded either in our use of worldly techniques because, as the book of James says, a double-minded person is unstable and shouldn't expect to receive anything from the Lord (James 1:6–8).

The MacArthur Study Bible explains the renewal of our minds like this: Salvation involves the mind (Romans 12:2; 2 Corinthians 10:5), which is the center of thought, understanding, and belief, as well as of motive and action (Colossians 3:1–2, 10). When a person becomes a Christian, God gives them a completely new moral and spiritual capability that a mind apart from Christ can never achieve.[31]

Now, can these things I am teaching help the non-Christian? I don't have an answer for that because it hasn't been my experience. Everyone I have taught is already a Christian or was converted shortly after. The things in this book are universal truths proven through science and corroborated with the Bible.

---

[31] John F. MacArthur, *The MacArthur Study Bible*, NIV (Thomas Nelson, 2015).

Is there a possibility that you can find lasting healing without the implementation of Scripture and outside the redemptive nature of God's love and salvation through Jesus Christ? Perhaps, but all the research I have done on the subject tells me quite the contrary. Any program or therapy outside the application of God's love will leave you unfulfilled and wounded. These other methods are only temporary solutions that mask the symptoms of our wound and never heal the deep infection of sin that plagues our existence.

Even this award-winning program utilized without the covering of God's love through the sacrifice of Jesus Christ will have only limited success in overcoming the trauma you have experienced.

So now we have walked awhile together, and I have been able to show you how the brain works and how our negative bias causes us to focus on irrational things. We have shown how Scripture teaches us how to overcome these things, and we have done exercises that prove the point. Now is a good time to pause and consider all we have learned together and ask yourself if you are ready to step into the next evolution of your healing process.

Along this path there are many fundamental shifts in your way of thinking, but none will be more important than this one.

Do you accept that Jesus was the Son of God, lived a sinless life, and died on the cross to bring salvation to all those who believe in Him?

Do you believe in your heart that He arose from the grave three days later, overcoming death, and ascended to heaven to sit at the right hand of God?

If you answer yes to these two questions, then you have just learned the gospel and now are ready to be forgiven of sin and find salvation through Jesus Christ.

The process is simple. Read these next few words and then pray them out loud to God: *Father, forgive me of my sins, and I am ready to receive salvation through the sacrifice of your son Jesus Christ.*

Now, these words are meaningless if you do not truly believe them when you say them. You must love God with all your heart, mind, body, and soul. This is the way to true salvation.

Optional: During the next few days I want you to write your own prayer—a prayer specific to your life. Structure it in a way that first gives thanks for a blessing you have received. Second, ask for the specific needs in your life, but ask with the expectation of receiving and a heart of thanksgiving. Third, close with a phrase of appreciation for grace.

Tactical Application

What you focus on, you will find more of. If you focus on problems, you will find more of them. What if you were to focus on solutions?

So let's look at the concept of negative bias again. Where do we have a negative bias? This may be hard to narrow down for most people, so I've found it easier to start with the things we avoid. Psychologically speaking, our negative bias rules our avoidance behavior. We do not know how to recognize it because we've never been looking for it before.

There is an old story about Columbus discovering the New World. It's a story, but myth would probably be more accurate. I heard it somewhere before, but its origin seems to come from a journal of a cook named John Banks in April 1770. The story comes from an expedition to Australia and here has been adapted to fit the discovery of the Americas. The tale goes something like this. At first, the natives could not see Spanish ships. It is said that they noticed a disturbance in the water but could not see the massive fleet. They called down the elders of the tribe to assess the waters. The elders looked for some time and finally announced to the tribe that there were large sailing vessels on the water causing the disturbance in the water. In his journal, Banks recalls watching the natives go about their daily routine completely oblivious to the presence of the large ships.[32]

[32] "James Cook (1728–1779): Pioneer of Scientific Exploration." *Endeavour*, vol. 2,

So why could the tribesmen only see the disturbance and not the ships? It is theorized that they could see the effects of the ships on the water but not the cause because they had never seen such large ships before. They had no frame of reference for a sailing vessel of that magnitude. Therefore, their brains could not make sense of what they were seeing, and they dismissed it as if it weren't there. In the same manner, it is difficult for us to recognize things in our lives that we have never experienced before. We are conditioned to look for things we recognize, but not the other way around. What you focus on, you will find more of.

Let's do an experiment. Study the image below for fifteen seconds. Quickly count how many gray flags you see. Write the number down.

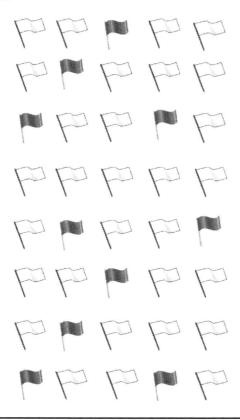

no. 3 (1978): 103, https://fdocuments.in/document/james-cook-17281779-pioneer-of-scientific-exploration.html.

How many gray flags?

How many white flags?

You didn't notice the white ones because you were focused on the gray flags. Isn't that how our brain works? We only saw what we focused on. The white flags were there the whole time, and there were even more of them, but we only focused on the gray ones. What we focus on, we see more of.

Think back to when you bought your truck, a blue Toyota Tacoma. Suddenly, you started seeing other blue Toyota Tacomas, Tacomas in other colors, and even other Toyotas. They seemed to be everywhere. Where did they all come from? They were there the whole time; you just hadn't paid any attention to them before. Once you owned one, your brain recognized them, connected with them, and categorized them.

What you focus on, you will find more of. If you focus on problems, you will find more of them. What if you were to focus on solutions? That's right—you will find more solutions. Be mindful of the things you focus on.

Your thoughts are a conversation with yourself overheard by the ears of God. Maybe it's time to change the conversation! Let's try that now. Look back over the journal you've been keeping at some of the things you've written. Where's your negative bias? What have you been avoiding? Be sure to take some time with this as you will need it in the subsequent chapters. You may find there are many, so write them all down, but for this exercise choose one "lie" that you tell yourself. Unpack it and reframe it. Once you learn how to do this, you can transfer the process to the others.

Debrief

I bet you're wondering why you weren't taught about negative bias in school. It sure could have saved a lot of trouble growing up. Knowing about it now allows you to take steps to overcome it. With posttraumatic stress, the negative bias has been supercharged and given full access to override rational thought. We—you and I—must take back control of this rebel so we can live a more peaceable life. Understanding the operations of the brain will help considerably with the healing process.

God took me on a journey of self-realization, and I have spent years poring over medical journals and research studies, as well as biblical principles, to understand how to heal from the effects of war. Fortunately, you will not have to spend ten years of trial and error. I have done my best to encompass this research into these pages to give you a jump-start on healing. We have got you up to speed on the functions of the brain so you will better understand them and accept them as truth. It's difficult for us to recognize things in our lives that we've never experienced before.

When I was in ANGLICO, the Air Naval Gunfire Liaison Company, I was trained as a forward observer. We had a very specific and highly sought-after skill set on the battlefield. We would parachute into hostile territory or be attached to forward elements to command the battlefield with close air support artillery and naval gunfire. Short of a nuclear option, there is no more destructive force on the battlefield than the forward observer and his radio.

I was already trained as a communications specialist, so my task training consisted of becoming not just proficient, but an expert at target identification, acquisition, and destruction. At first this was a difficult task. Target identification was the beginning of my training. We would look at terrain photos and try to identify targets, defining friend and foe. I had no idea what I was looking for. I had been in the Marines less than a year and had very little exposure to our military vehicles. Making it more difficult, I didn't have a childhood where the military was ever talked about. I didn't have any military-style toys or action figures growing up, except for a few plastic green army men, and those were the knockoff brand.

When it came to finding targets in terrain photos or sitting on an observation post, I was lost. I had no frame of reference. My brain had nothing to corroborate objects I saw that were partially obscured or camouflaged. It wasn't until they gave us flash cards with the silhouettes of vehicles that I could begin to pick them out. I couldn't recognize something I had never seen, even though it was right in front of me. It took a lot of time to condition my brain before I could acquire targets, but once I had it, I never lost it. Even to this day, I can scan the terrain of a mountain or a cityscape and pick out anomalies. My brain has been conditioned to the point of automation. I can look at almost any environment and pick out the things others miss.

If we can agree that our mind can negatively affect our body, could it be taught to work positively as well? From the Word of God, and from my training in the military, I know these things are possible. We can condition our brain to find what we're looking for. The key is to look for the right things. Keep this in mind as we outline the process called Healing thru Service.

CHAPTER 6
AMYGDALA HIJACK:
FIGHT, FLIGHT, FREEZE

Imminent Threat + Subconscious = Survival
Perceived Threat + Subconscious = Panic

Personal Recon

I VIVIDLY REMEMBER A TIME I was driving west on the Maple Valley Highway. This highway is a two-lane road winding through the hills near Cedar River that I had driven thousands of times. The river was off to my right, and the cliff face of the mountain was on my left. There is no shoulder on either side of this stretch of road.

The area is prone to mudslides, and traffic is always difficult. I was driving at normal speed when a dump truck approached in the oncoming lane. I immediately focused on my driving speed and lane position. I crept slowly toward the fog line to allow the large truck a wide berth.

As the truck passed, I heard a loud explosion, and debris peppered my windshield on the driver's side. In an instant, I was transported back to Iraq. I punched the gas and began taking evasive maneuvers. I honestly could not tell you what happened in the next few moments, but when I came back to reality, I noticed I was death-gripping the steering wheel and yelling commands to people who weren't there. Yelling commands in an empty vehicle. *What the hell am I doing?* I thought, *And where am I?* I had traveled several miles down the road with no recollection of the past few moments. I looked at the speedometer, and I was tacking out at 80 miles per hour.

As my conscious mind came back online, I was flooded with emotion and the chemicals my brain was releasing. I began to shake and feel sick. The sudden surge of adrenaline and cortisol was having full effect on me. I felt nauseated, and my head was swimming in a fog of very raw emotions. I had to fight for what I thought was reality and focus my mind on the task at hand—driving. By this point, the road had turned into four lanes with a small shoulder on the right.

I pulled over and got out of the car. As I attempted to walk, my legs went weak, and I had to steady myself against my car to stay up. The chemicals released by my brain into my veins were severely compromising my mind and now my body. I could see the guardrail just ahead and staggered toward it. I straddled the guardrail and toppled over it onto the grass. I couldn't catch my breath as I knelt, bent over on my hands and knees. I noticed I was making a weird growling noise as I tried to breathe; it was strange, almost guttural, like a strange creature was trying to escape from behind my teeth. I flopped onto my side and slowly rolled onto my back. As I looked up, I could feel the warmth of the sun on my face and the leaves of the trees blowing in the wind just above me. I lay there in the grass for what had to be twenty minutes, trying to calm myself. What the heck had just happened? I would later learn that this is what is known as an amygdala hijack, more commonly known as a panic attack.

As I lay there, I mentally recalled the events that had just happened. Later, I realized that the sound I heard was the truck's tire blowing out, and the debris was bits of the tire hitting my car. Although frightening, this triggered a panic response far beyond what an average driver would experience. Through the practice of a process I call SRD (Structure, Routine, and Discipline), I've been able to overcome these incidents with a higher probability of success. As you continue through this book, I will pass these skills on to you. However, these tools only work if you use them.

Field Intel

> *It is your most primal part of the brain. When it takes*
> *over, you are in a state of amygdala hijack. It can save*
> *your life, but can also hinder you, because*
> *there is no off switch.*
> —Sgt Q

Anxiety and panic attacks occur when our subconscious mind attempts to take control of our conscious mind, bombarding the conscious mind with so much intel that it can't make sense of reality. Even though the conscious sees the intel the subconscious presents, it shuts down, allowing the subconscious to take over. At this moment, cognitive thoughts and abilities cease, and we go into survival mode. Once in survival mode, our bodies default to the three *F*s: flight, fight, and freeze. These three choices are all the subconscious has to work with. Again, the subconscious has limited capacity for reasonable thought. This mechanism is great if there's an actual threat. However, when the threat is only perceived and not a reality, the effects can be extremely detrimental. Here is what it might look like as a formula:

$$\text{Imminent Threat} + \text{Subconscious} = \text{Survival}$$
$$\text{Perceived Threat} + \text{Subconscious} = \text{Panic}$$

The medical term for this state of flight, fight, and freeze is the *amygdala hijack*. This condition is an immediate, overwhelming emotional response followed by the realization that the response was inappropriately strong, given the trigger. Daniel Goleman coined the term based on the work of neuroscientist Joseph LeDoux.[33] LeDoux demonstrated that some emotional information travels directly from the thalamus to the amygdala without engaging the neocortex, or the higher brain regions. This causes a strong emotional response that supersedes more rational thought.

So how do we combat this hijack of our mental state and emotions? We control the subconscious mind by manipulating the information it gives us. We allow our conscious mind to do its job and process the information provided by our subconscious. Once we know how the brain functions and how each side operates, we can learn to live better. Just like everything in life, the rewards will not be given to us. We must be relentless in our pursuit of a stable equilibrium.

When I first started my journey with posttraumatic stress treatment, I read a lot about how the brain works and the different functions of the mind. I studied the effects of medication and of cognitive therapy, and I embraced the introduction of meditation and prayer. I pored over journals related to different mental disorders and alternate therapies. What I am about to teach you has been the treatment I developed for myself over the last decade. These skills and tools have served me well, and my hope is that they

[33] Monty McKeever, "The Brain and Emotional Intelligence: An Interview with Daniel Goleman," *Daniel Goleman*, video interview, May 19, 2011, www.danielgoleman.info/the-brain-and-emotional-intelligence-an-interview-with-daniel-goleman/.

will lessen the learning curve as you face your battle with posttraumatic stress. I'm not a miracle worker, and this is not a cure. I do not offer one, but what I can offer is a way to live with this condition and have a healthy and successful life filled with solace and joy.

In the veteran community, we don't like the label of PTSD. The "D" stands for and suggests we have a disorder—it's a label that can be damaging in and of itself. You may have recognized that I've only referred to posttraumatic stress in previous chapters. This label of posttraumatic stress has taken on its own stereotype. We have all battled the label, so by attempting to change the narrative and just using the term posttraumatic stress, we are one step closer to managing its effects. God has spent the last several years teaching me these lessons, and now I'm teaching them to you. Retrain your brain to tell the subconscious what you want it to show you, and recategorize it into a usable neural pathway that brings growth and hope to your life.

When a loud noise startles you, your subconscious automatically floods your conscious mind with a warning of doom, and you feel desperate to get out of the situation, desperate to survive. The main function of the subconscious is to preserve life, to survive whatever threat may be near—even if it is only a perceived threat. It cannot see the reality that you are safe and the noise should not be alarming. The very small part of your brain, a physical part, called the amygdala, is your brain's most primal part. When it takes over, you are in a state of amygdala hijack. It can save your life, but can also be a hindrance, because there is no off switch.

So how do you use this information? I found that I could talk myself down, literally. I remind myself that I am safe; the noise was just someone dropping something. I go through my function check. I reassure myself that everything is okay. I focus on the positive things around me. I am with my brothers, I am with warriors, I am helping others, the sun is shining on my face. It seems odd at first, but the more you practice, the easier it becomes and the quicker you can bring yourself back from the edge.

Scripture Unpack

Fear is the foe that will keep you living a timid and unin-
spired life. But you can capture that fear, harness its raw
power, and ride it like the wind on to victory. Fear that is
controlled is the most powerful catalyst for change.
—Sgt Q

God did not give you a spirit of fear. Fear can keep you from a lot of things, but you can harness that fear and ride it like the wind on to victory. For a long time, I allowed fear to control my life and keep me from my destiny. This is a problem I've had ever since returning from Iraq. I would worry and stress over every decision I made. It used to be a crippling issue for me, and it would always give way to a panic attack. I didn't have the problem before the war. I was a go-getter.

I joined the Marines as a seventeen-year-old, five-foot-five-inch, 125-pound teenager full of piss and vinegar. I purposely joined the toughest military branch in the world. People would often look at me sideways when they found out I joined. It was a look of *Are you sure that's a good idea?*

I guess I never really noticed my small stature, but as I look at my sixteen-year-old son, who is the same size I was when I joined, I now know why people looked at me funny. I often wonder how I made it. How was I able to join 1st ANGLICO and become a master parachutist and close combat instructor? It was because I had no fear, no worries. I never doubted I could do it. Nothing seemed impossible for me. People would stand around and talk about doing something, but I was the guy who just jumped in and started doing it. I'm not sure why. I'm wired that way, I guess.

I remember driving to main side with my sergeant. While we were there, CamelBak was doing a demo for the hydration packs we carried. They were doing a push-up competition, and you could win a CamelBak if you placed in the top three. There was a crowd of Marines standing around watching two or three guys pump out reps. They were all talking about the two or three guys participating. They bragged about how they would do it differently or how they could do more than the other guys, but they weren't going to try because they had already lifted for the day. Blah blah blah. I stood around for about a minute before joining the competition. It was simple—whoever could do the most push-ups without quitting. You could rest, but only the front leaning rest or the push-up position. When all was said and done, I did 217 consecutive push-ups and won a CamelBak. I still have it today and take it with me on the mission field sometimes. Think about that—217 push-ups! How many of us could do fifty, or even twenty, right now? Looking back, I even have a hard time believing I did it. No fear—I never doubted I could do it, and I knew I would win.

That all changed when I came back from deployment. Anxiety, panic attacks, and nightmares began to slowly chip away at my self-confidence. I no longer felt invincible. I began to question myself. I would question every choice I made and then run it over and over in my mind until I completely shut down.

I don't know if you do the same thing. I don't know if you lost that fearless side of yourself, but if you did—getting it back will be a long, arduous journey filled with highs and lows. I still haven't regained that same fearlessness. I am still afraid when I do most anything. Leading teams on the mission field, presenting Operation Restore Hope, or even going to a grocery store can and does often strike the fear chord in my heart. I will second-guess myself. I will lie awake in the early mornings, worried I won't be able to perform. I'll ask myself, *Why am I doing all this? Why don't I just quit and walk away?*

The fear of failure is a heavy burden. Before Iraq, there were no real consequences for failure. But in Iraq, failure meant death. This became all too real on deployment. I guess that's why I am so afraid of it now. This is a revelation I'm making for the first time. It's strange to share it with you in its raw form—a thought that reveals a darker part of myself I didn't know was there.

In my research of *fear* in the Bible, I found that almost every person going on mission for God had to overcome this spirit of fear. It is an old foe that has plagued mankind since the garden of Eden. Fear is what caused Adam to hide from God when he sinned. Fear kept Moses from confronting the pharaoh by himself. He only decided to go if his brother Aaron could accompany him. Fear gripped the Israelites when they laid eyes on the walls of Jericho. The disciples of Jesus felt fear in the garden of Gethsemane when the soldiers came to capture Jesus before going to His death on the cross. Fear is the foe that will keep you living a timid and uninspired life. But you can capture your fear, harness its raw power, and ride it like the wind on to victory. Fear that is controlled is the most powerful catalyst for change. It's like NOS for your '69 Nova or a booster to your Falcon heavy rocket. How do we reign in this power? Let's consult Scripture: "For God has not given us a spirit of fear, but of power and of love and of a sound mind" (2 Timothy 1:7 NKJV).

This is Paul writing to Timothy to encourage him as he went out to preach the gospel. He knew Timothy was afraid, but Timothy went anyway. I still do things. I still accomplish goals, but I am almost always afraid when I do it. I used to think I was brave because I was fearless. Now I know true bravery is being afraid and moving forward anyway. Let's look a little deeper.

"For God has not given us a spirit of *fear*, but of power and of love and of a sound mind." The original word used here translates as *pusillanimous*, often translated as *cowardice*. God did not give us a spirit of cowardice, which makes sense because we are created in His image. Knowing this, we must assume that we are all born to be bold warriors for the gospel.

I have said before that you do not have to be a Christian to use these principles, although I believe it is far more helpful. Just as I am leading you through this path of healing, the Holy Spirit leads you through many more trials as you follow Jesus Christ in faith. From here on out, our two paths diverge—that of the believer and that of the nonbeliever. I cannot say for certain that the nonbeliever will receive the full benefits of the teaching past this point, but I am hopeful. I am also praying for the nonbeliever at some point to desire to receive the gift of salvation offered to all mankind through the blood of Jesus Christ and His sacrifice for us.

No matter which path you take, you are still welcome to continue this journey. Just know that some of these teachings may not be fully comprehensible unless the Holy Spirit is with you, because it's the Holy Spirit who teaches spiritual truths to those who are spiritual and belong to Jesus Christ (1 Corinthians 2:10–13).

When Jesus is with you, you have access to a whole different view of reality and a whole other set of weapons for your arsenal. One of the most important weapons is the shield of faith. I use this most often when battling the effects of posttraumatic stress. My faith in Jesus Christ protects me from the enemy's attacks, but fear still overwhelms me at times. Even to this day, I must fight back the panic response. Most times I am successful, but sometimes I fail. I am happy to report that I have many more in the win column because I have learned the process taught in this chapter, and because of how I now see the world.

Sometimes the world can become distorted. There is so much stimuli coming in that my brain can't process it, and I can only see what's in front of me. It's hard to explain, but it's like I shut out everything else and can only focus on what's in front of me. When I become hyperfocused on the fear, it overtakes me. The days before I deploy on a mission are the hardest for me. I pack my bags and load my tools. They are staged by the door. All my clothes are ranger rolled and tightly packed to save room. My three most important tools are inventoried: my med kit—check; my pocketknife—check; and my traveling Bible—check. I have taken the same small brown leather-back Bible on every mission. It is light and travels well. It is the most important part of my kit. Nothing left to do but get some rack time before the outward push in the morning.

Regardless of how well I prepare, these are the hardest days. My body feels off center and just not quite right. There's a sickness in my gut that burns like I swallowed a hot coal. And there's a lump in my throat that's so big it feels like I could choke on it. My emotions run high. It feels like I could cry at any moment for any reason. I am full of nervous excitement—the same feeling you may have got readying your kit to move outside the wire. Or the feeling when you hear the jumpmaster yell, "One minute," and the door of the bird slides open, exposing the distant earth below—and there's the rush of the wind on your face and the smell of jet fuel mixed with vomit that fills the air, and the knot in your stomach feels as big as a watermelon. "Thirty seconds!" My body begs me to stay, but I know I must press on. I know I must get on that plane in the morning.

This is the mission God has given me. This is my life now. Most would not go. I don't blame them. Especially if their body betrayed them as mine has done. We live in the greatest country in the world, so why would anyone want to leave all the comforts of home and endure hardship? It is countercultural. Everyone wants to come to America, not leave it. I guess God wired some of us differently. When people hear chaos and violence, it is natural to run from it. But some of us have trained our bodies to suppress their natural survival instinct and run toward the danger. The red light turns to green, and the jumpmaster yells, "Go!"

We have mastered this fear, and we ride it toward the sounds of chaos—not away from it. I will take down my lamp from its stand and push forward into the darkness of my soul, because it is in the darkness that fear lies, and I must destroy it before it destroys me. I don't know how to overcome these feelings. I just push through them until I'm on the other side. I'm not sure if the night will be restless or full of worry and nightmares. Although the stress may overcome me in the moment, I know that with the light of a new day, my hope will be restored. I will grab my gear and make for the plane.

The only way to get over fear is to go straight through it—just do it afraid. You can harness the power of fear by finding comfort in the Scriptures. One of the many reasons I love the Bible is because there are specific portions that were written to the warrior class. Written by warriors for warriors. There are things in there that warriors will understand on a whole different level. My favorite of these verses is in Psalm 91. The author expands on our mortal fear, expresses how God is our fortress, and concludes that we can take refuge in Him. The Bible is littered with references to the battlefield, the warriors, and God as our refuge, our high tower, our protector. For those of us who have served and now follow Christ, the Bible comes alive in a new way. There are references to warfare in here that can only be truly appreciated by the warrior mind. Psalm 91:1–16 (KJV 2000) assures us there is no fear for those abiding in God:

> He that dwells in the secret place of the most High shall abide under the shadow of the Almighty.
> I will say of the LORD, He is my refuge and my fortress: my God; in him will I trust.
> Surely he shall deliver you from the snare of the fowler, and from the deadly pestilence.
> He shall cover you with his feathers, and under his wings shall you trust; his truth shall be your shield and buckler.
> You shall not be afraid for the terror by night; nor for the arrow that flies by day;
> Nor for the pestilence that walks in darkness; nor for the destruction that wastes at noonday.
> A thousand shall fall at your side, and ten thousand at your right hand; but it shall not come near you.
> Only with your eyes shall you behold and see the reward of the wicked.
> Because you have made the LORD, who is my refuge,

even the most High, your habitation;

There shall no evil befall you, neither shall any plague
come near your dwelling.

For he shall give his angels charge over you, to keep you
in all your ways.

They shall bear you up in their hands, lest you dash your
foot against a stone.

You shall tread upon the lion and adder: the young lion
and the serpent shall you trample under feet.

Because he has set his love upon me, therefore will I
deliver him: I will set him on high, because he has
known my name.

He shall call upon me, and I will answer him: I will be
with him in trouble; I will deliver him, and honor
him.

With long life will I satisfy him, and show him my salvation.

Who wrote this psalm? Some say it was David, but others say Moses. No one knows for sure, but it's clear the author was a warrior. It was someone who understood the battlefield tactics and relayed God's love for His people through the lessons he learned and what he saw on the battlefield. John MacArthur describes it like this: "The Psalm describes God's ongoing sovereign protection of his people from ever-present danger and terrors which surround humanity. The original setting may be that of an army about to go into battle."[34]

I believe the Bible was written to all believers, but there's something extra for warriors like us. There are gems written by warriors for warriors. There are things that we may understand just a little more clearly. Words like *refuge*, *fortress*, *shield*, and *buckler* hold a deeper meaning to those who have wielded them in battle. The

[34] John MacArthur, *The MacArthur Bible Commentary* (Thomas Nelson, 2005), 658.

terrors at night and the arrows by day (Psalm 91:5): This Scripture is for those of us who have been on a night patrol or stood post where the darkness was our biggest enemy, always believing there was someone lurking just beyond the reach of the light, cloaked among the shadows waiting for their opportunity to devour us. We have seen the rain of gunfire and heard the sick whine of an inbound mortar—the arrows by day.

Most people are well versed, or at least think they are, about warfare. When it comes to spiritual warfare, not so much. This is a very in-depth subject and one that warrants a book of its own. Who knows—I may write it someday. Maybe you will. For now, spend time in prayer and fasting. Study the Word and remain honorable in all things.

We all struggle with fear, so do not get down on yourself because you feel weak and experience a lack of boldness from time to time. We all do. Even two of Jesus's disciples experienced fear and shrank in the face of danger. If you read Acts 2:14–41, you'll see how even those who walked with Jesus failed to have courage. So do not lose heart if right now you have less courage than you would like. When fear and panic grab you by the throat and fling you into the backseat of your life, only with practice will you be able to take back control of these situations.

Tactical Application

Those who don't assess never change, they never grow, and they never get past their current mental state.

—Sgt Q

The first exercise we will do in this section I have used for years. I cannot take credit for creating it, and I am not quite sure where I picked it up from. It had to be from one of those medical or psychology journals I read, but I can't nail down which one to give you as a specific resource. If you do a quick search on the internet, you'll find a variety of websites that use this technique, so it's well vetted and becoming common practice. You use it when you're in the middle of a panic attack and want to come out of it quickly. I've had success using it and leading others through it. It can be difficult to remember to do when you're in the midst of a panic attack, so if you have a spouse or roommate, it may be good to have them ask you these questions until you get into the habit of doing it yourself.

The goal of the next exercise is to create a pathway for the conscious mind to come back to reality while suppressing your subconscious reactions. Having to recognize things in your environment jump-starts the logic and reasoning portions of your brain, while at the same time directing the subconscious mind to give you information you need. This delays the negative bias and amygdala response. Remember, the subconscious mind is constantly taking in information from its environment, sorting and sending relevant information to the conscious mind to assist with our decision-making process. By directing the subconscious to give us information, we take back control of our mind and its operations.

Exercises

1. Grounding techniques

These are good techniques to use to overcome those sudden panic attacks. They force you to control the information your subconscious mind produces, putting your conscious mind back in control of your body (see INTEL for a deeper look at how the brain works).

Name five things you can see.
Name four things you can feel.
Name three things you can hear.
Name two things you can smell.
Name one thing you admire about yourself.

You must become adept at knowing what your body is telling you. Pay close attention to any changes in your mood, temperature, breathing, or other sensations in your body. These are warning signs. Through trial and error, you will begin to recognize them.

2. Stop–Look–Listen.

We all have sudden panic attacks or feelings of uneasiness. We need to learn to recognize the signs and sensations in our bodies so we can battle the panic before it achieves maximum impact. For me, I can feel the stress hormones coursing through my veins. I know when I need to start talking myself down and when I must do it fast.

Think back to your training. What did the military teach you to do when on patrol? During my time in 1st ANGLICO, we employed a wide variety of tactics on the battlefield. The most important of these was to pay close attention to our surroundings when on the move or in a static environment. Small changes in the AO (area of operation) could yield dramatic signals of impending dangers. We were taught to Stop–Look–Listen. On patrol, we would come to a danger area, a road crossing, a building, a wide-open area, or a choke point and would halt the patrol (Stop). Every man would face outward and look for small anomalies in the terrain. It could be fresh footprints or drag marks, equipment or debris, or anything that looked out of place that signaled troop movements, IEDs, or ambushes. We would scan in sectors. First from a foot to a meter out, from left to right, then again ten meters out, left to right, twenty meters, fifty meters, and so on until we had surveyed the entire area for anything suspicious (Look). We would regulate our breathing and heart rate. We would listen for anything in the area, any sound, trying to identify it as natural or unnatural, friend or foe (Listen).

This technique was valuable for an ANGLICO team of four to eight men that usually operated with limited reinforcement separated from a larger combat element. If compromised, we would be on our own. We had to be immensely more cautious as a small team because a regular enemy patrol could easily overrun us. Stop–Look–Listen was valuable to avoid enemy contact and could be initiated at any time if something didn't feel quite right.

I have repurposed the same Stop–Look–Listen tactic to avoid panic attacks. I have learned to pay close attention to how my body feels. The function check is the tool I use. I have become very adept at this and am now able to consciously recognize the signals my subconscious is sending out. This allows my conscious mind to rationally evaluate these changes in my environment and take appropriate action or to use my grounding techniques to override the impending amygdala hijack.

Stop. When you notice something, stop what you are doing.

Look. Scan your environment to see what, if anything, is triggering you. Is the room too hot? Did a suspicious person enter the room? Is the area crowded?

Listen. Listen to what your body is telling you. Recognize the sensations you're having and the thoughts you're experiencing. Did your heart rate increase? Your mouth get dry? Your stomach turn upside down?

Using these techniques will dramatically increase your ability to recognize your posttraumatic stress triggers before they become a panic attack. We will explore what to do once we have identified these triggers, and we will learn how we can use this information to build a battle plan to overcome the spirit of fear and shut down the amygdala hijack. For now, focus on being present in the moment, and engage your conscious mind. Recognize when things feel off, and investigate the cause.

Debrief

John Gill, a renowned English Baptist pastor, said that with fear comes a snare.[35] Doesn't it feel like that at times? Doesn't it

---

[35] John Gill, "Proverbs 29:25," *John Gill's Exposition of the Bible*, Bible Study Tools, https://www.biblestudytools.com/commentaries/gills-exposition-of-the-bible/proverbs-29-25.html.

feel like we're caught in a trap in our mind, stuck in a pit we can't seem to escape? Using these techniques, and becoming proficient at them, will allow you not only to get out of that trap, but will teach you how to avoid the trap altogether. Now don't be discouraged if you find yourself stuck in a trap, having a panic attack, or the like. It's fine; it still happens to me from time to time, but becoming better at recognizing them is how we cope.

The most important tactic is to unpack the experience as soon as you can. Similar to after an engagement, do your after actions report. You look at what went right and what went wrong. Take note of these things so you can use them later. Most people would rather not think of their failures or look back over their behavior because that can be embarrassing to them. Those who don't assess never change, they never grow, and they never get past their current mental state.

The US military is so formidable on the battlefield for this reason. When we rigorously break down every aspect of each operation's shortcoming, we can then reinforce positions and replicate successes in future missions. By dissecting our last posttraumatic stress episode, we can see where we went sideways and make preparations for the next time. By taking the time to self-evaluate and sift through the ashes of past mistakes and hardships, we will gather valuable information that we can use to grow stronger; therefore, we can avoid making the same mistakes. Like the phoenix, we can rise from the ashes of our past and evolve into someone more powerful and self-aware.

CHAPTER 7

CHANGE YOUR THINKING, CHANGE YOUR LIFE, CREATE A NEW NEURAL PATHWAY

*. . . an internal conflict that would ravage my body from
the inside out.*
—Sgt Q

Personal Recon

WHEN I WAS TWELVE YEARS OLD, I was homeless with my mom and
three sisters. We lived along a river in northern California for several months. When you are a kid and homeless, you don't truly

understand it. You don't know exactly what's going on, but you know it's not right. My mom did the best she could for us. She left an abusive relationship with my dad. She had nowhere to go and no one to help her. She took us all to the river, and we lived in tents; "camping," she called it. I believe she called it camping partly to protect us from knowing we were homeless, and partly to protect herself from the grim reality of being a single mom with four young kids—with no job, no home, and no hope. It was a dire situation.

I remember spending most of my time trying to visit friends and ignoring the fact that we didn't have a place to call our own. She eventually decided to move us to Oregon, where she found work as a maid. We stayed with friends until she could move us into a small one-bedroom house. It was tight for a family of five, but it was warm and dry, and it was enough. Still, to this day, my mom shudders any time the subject is brought up.

Later in life, I found myself homeless again. This time it was eight months after coming back from Iraq. At the time, I didn't understand my posttraumatic stress, and I wasn't able to sustain a job or any semblance of a relationship. I found myself living mostly in my car or couch surfing, between Oregon and California. I would sell drugs along the way to make some cash to keep me going, sending what I could to my ex-wife and kids. I was truly lost at this point.

After turning my life around and coming out of homelessness, I was terrified to go back. It was my primary fear. For most of the war, I was by myself at an observation post, able to see everyone and everything, but not able to be a part of the unit. Homelessness is a lot like that—on the fringe of society, but unable to fully participate. It wasn't until much later that I figured out my mind had connected the two events in my life. Anytime I experienced financial difficulty, I would have a panic attack, and my subconscious would take over in a futile attempt to preserve life. This would lead to a cycle of anxiety, depression, and suicidal thoughts, then anger, regret, loss, and more anxiety.

My fear of homelessness and abandonment was so great that it would override all other common-sense decisions. My go-to feelings would be anger and hurt—anger and hurt that God would allow me as a child to experience homelessness, and then after serving my country honorably and faithfully, to find myself once again facing homelessness. This was such a struggle for me; it was an internal conflict that ravaged my body from the inside out. I wasn't able to overcome it until I learned to face the fear. I realized I had a choice. I could continue to live in fear and be angry about my past, or I could use that experience to propel myself forward to help others in the way I was hoping someone would help me.

During my time of homelessness and suffering through posttraumatic stress, I longed for a hero to come and rescue me from the situation. The hero never came, so now I'm going to be that hero for someone else, and you can do the same thing. You can help others through their pain and use your life experience to lead them. You don't have to have it all together; you just have to let Christ lead you. I still have to choose to be that hero year after year building houses for the homeless. I do it because I've felt the pain and insecurity of homelessness. The trials I experienced taught me to reframe the greatest obstacle in my life into an opportunity. This hardship I've encountered has given me compassion for the homeless. Genesis 50:20 tells us that what the enemy means for evil, God will use for the good of His people. I now hold tight to this promise.

This was not the case at first, for in the beginning I was bitter about my situation. It wasn't until I faced my fear and built my first home in Mexico with Pastor Loran that I began my journey of healing—an incredible, action-packed adventure of Healing thru Service. By the end of this book, you, too, will have all the tools necessary to step out on your own journey of healing through serving others. It was along this path that I realized God had a plan for my life all along. He has a plan for yours too.

Let's pause here for a moment and prepare some things that you will need in the next chapter. Think briefly of an encounter or experience that brings you pain when your mind wanders. It doesn't have to be the most traumatic thing you've gone through, but it should be something that invokes a physical sensation in your body or an immediate shutdown of the memory, like how a computer program crashes because of corrupt data. Think of it as if you were touching a hot stove. You immediately pull away from the stove because it causes real pain—just like you want to pull away from the memory because it causes pain. You may even notice a physical reaction like a small body shudder or the shaking of the head to somehow shake loose the memory from your consciousness. That's what we're looking for. Let's start with something small. I'm sure by now there are hundreds spinning around in your mind—the hurts, pains, and memories you want to forget, to push away, and never have to deal with. You know the type—the subconscious files in the "never deal with—*never*" box.

Let's pluck one of the low-hanging fruits. Take a moment to write it down. We do not need the full story with all the details, just one or two sentences that will make it easy to recall. Be mindful not to get SOS here—it's easy to do. Recognize it and use the skills you learned earlier to bring the subconscious back under control and continue cognitive thought.

Field Intel

> *Our brain wants to connect the dots to create a strong neural network. We do not have to be a passive rider on this roller coaster of life. We have the ability to choose our own path on this neural network of brain synapses and firing peptides.*
> —Sgt Q

Let's look back at our simple example of the two-part brain. While the brain and our mind are far more miraculous and complex than we can fathom, a simple model can help us grasp the essentials. Think of the conscious and the subconscious as two people sitting opposite each other at a desk. The subconscious is facing the wall but has access to all the filing cabinets with all the saved information about everything that's happened. He faces the wall and can't see the outside reality. The information he puts on the desk becomes his reality. The conscious mind sits opposite the subconscious and only has access to the info the subconscious puts on top of the desk, but he can see through the windows behind and out of the sight of the subconscious. What the conscious sees out the window is the reality we all share. Of course, it is far more complex, but this simplification can help us think about our situation.

Most people know of only two ways to deal with the intel their subconscious gives them: deal with it or dismiss it. When we deal with the thought or memory given to us by the subconscious, we decide how to react based on the intel provided. The subconscious will then note the results and file the intel back in the filing cabinet. When we dismiss the intel, it's the equivalent of flinging all the papers off the desk. This is when we shut down the memory and push it away. I'm sure you've experienced this; I know I sure have.

The subconscious is not happy with this sort of reaction, and it files it in a box labeled "deal with it later." You *will* deal with it later, trust me. The subconscious will at some point have enough of the avoidance, the room will fill from wall to wall with those boxes, and it will become increasingly difficult to function. Memory issues and concentration will suffer. The brain will start to shut down in a way similar to a computer having too many programs open at the same time, which diminishes the random-access memory (RAM) because it's too full. Everything runs slow or can freeze, and eventually it crashes. Our brain can have the same kind of experience if we spend our life jamming everything in the "deal with it later" box.

Have you seen those episodes of *Hoarders* on television? Hoarders are people living in a home packed with so much junk that they can't even move around. There are only narrow passageways to move from room to room. Usually, the kitchen and bathroom are so cluttered that there's no way to use them. The occupant's health deteriorates because they cannot properly groom themselves or prepare food. The clutter is so bad that no one will come to visit. The hoard becomes their only friend, and they become emotionally attached to something that causes them pain. The fear of losing those things overrides their desire to connect with people.

Sounds a lot like posttraumatic stress. We never deal with or let go of the painful memories, so they keep collecting until our mind is so burdened with them that it doesn't function properly. We can only think along narrow pathways, and our health and hygiene become compromised. People stop visiting and interacting. We become isolated and are embarrassed by our behavior, but the pain of dealing with those memories overrides our desire to connect with people. At a certain point, the subconscious will refuse to work correctly, and you will see malfunctions in systems that should be running normally—illness, depression, moodiness, interrupted sleep, and loss of sex drive, to name a few. The subconscious says, *If I can't happy, then nobody's happy*, and things grind to a halt.

Self-medication, addiction, and suicide can soon follow because our conscious mind is trying to drown out the subconscious mind, usually with some sort of addiction to drugs, alcohol, sex, or—you name it. I'm sure at this point some of you are reading this and saying, *This is me. Is this guy reading my mail? Is he in my head somehow?* You see, we have all had different experiences, but the truth is that we aren't that different when it comes to the basic structure of our brain and its central processing ability.

We all have a "deal with it later" box, but when we allow the room to become filled with these boxes, the subconscious has no room to function. It likes things neat and orderly, not cluttered. It wants to process and file all these thoughts and emotions. So your choices are to deal with the emotion, thought, or feeling, recognize it for what it is, glean some bit of knowledge from it, and file it away, *or* you can push the emotion down anytime the thought comes in order to avoid people, places, or things that remind you of the pain. Neither of these options is ideal, but what if there were a third option? What if you could reframe those hard memories and difficult emotions into empowerment? What if all those things you thought were holding you back were doing so only because you wouldn't let go of them?

I've learned how to reframe the intel and allow the subconscious to file it in a different area. Like I said, our brain wants to connect the dots to create a strong neural network. We do not have to be a passive rider on this roller coaster of life. We have the ability to choose our own path on this neural network of brain synapses and firing peptides. Where did this revelation come from? Where did I find out how to do this? I found it in the Bible. The Bible shows us how in James 1:2 (ESV): "Count it all joy, my brothers, when you meet trials of various kinds."

That is a simple verse, but it has far-reaching implications when it comes to the complex network of our brain and how it creates memories and changes the way we view the world in which we live. Let me help you break this down.

Scripture Unpack

"Count it all joy" (James 1:2 ESV).

- Count: check over one by one to determine
- It: direct representation of the trial
- All: the whole of collective; every experience
- Joy: emotion of great delight and happiness

Why does James tell us to count it all joy when we fall into various trials? He explains it in the next two verses: "For you know that the testing of your faith produces steadfastness. And let steadfastness have its full effect, that you may be perfect and complete, lacking in nothing" (James 1:3–4 ESV).

James is telling us that when we change our mindset to find joy in the midst of trials, we will be purifying our faith to perfection. In verse 12, he continues this thought when he says, "Blessed is the man who remains steadfast under trial, for when he has stood the test he will receive the crown of life, which God has promised to those who love him."

A few winters ago, I had a knife custom-made. As I went through the ordering process, I researched how raw metal was heated, refined, and shaped into a weapon. I learned great parallels between how the metal is tested and how we are tested. I had been tested and refined in the furnace of battle, but I had to let my metal go cold before I could begin knocking the slag off. Impurities that come out of the metal when it's exposed to high temperatures become slag and must be knocked off before the metal cools, or it will leave a hard, ugly blemish over the top of the beautiful refined metal. There is no way to remove this slag once the metal is cooled.

Isaiah 48:10 (NKJV) tells us, "Behold, I have refined you, but not as silver; I have tested you in the furnace of affliction." I have found fifteen other verses that compare the trials of our life to the refining furnace. God is showing us that these trials are to refine us, to take out the useless parts, to purify us. God allows us to be put in the furnace, but we must help knock off the slag. You must heat the metal again and knock off the slag by pounding the metal. This not only knocks off the slag, but it also shapes the metal.

- The furnace: a trial in our life that produces pain
- Slag: the pain left in our life because we refuse to deal with it

- Slag build-up: so much pain in our life that it covers our beauty. Slag sticks to slag, just as our hurts connect to others, even if they are not related.
- Reheat the furnace: open up the "deal with it later" box and knock off the slag. Reframing those hurts will free your pure metal, your pure spirit.

People look for those who have been through trials and gravitate toward them when they are faced with adversity. No one looks to the guy in shining armor for battle tactics. They look for the old scarred warrior with busted armor, chips in his shield, and blood on his blade. That is a man with a story to tell and lessons to teach.

Without realizing it, you are in the furnace right now. This book is designed to heat up your metal and knock off some slag. There are, no doubt, triggers that will pop up. Do not shove them back in the box. Take time to unpack them. Reframe them. Grow and become the person you are intended to be, free from the pain of past hurts, sorrows, and bitterness.

People call this finding the silver lining, making the best of a bad situation, or making lemonade when you have lemons. This is not a new concept I'm proposing. You just need to understand how to do it.

The University of California-Berkeley has studied this same concept. They have created an entire website dedicated to activities that help a person build these skills. You can find them here: https://ggia.berkeley.edu/about_us. The results and testimonies are remarkable. After I created my program, I consulted with mental health specialists and was given other research that falls in line with this type of cognitive therapy. There are others discovering the same information. The more you research how the brain works, the more you will understand yourself and how to cope with posttraumatic stress. Understanding how the brain functions is a complex endeavor. Consider this small, yet profound fact: The brain is the only thing that actually named itself.

I'll share with you an example from my own life of how to reframe your thoughts to stop a downward spiral and create a new connection and pathway to happiness. From this, you will gather the framework to do things in your own life with great success. What took me years to unpack and put together, you will do in an afternoon. I'm a slow learner, and I am confident you might be quicker. Remember this as we move forward: I cannot control what happens, but now I can control how I react to it.

Tactical Application

It is ingrained in us to focus on the negative aspect as a survival instinct. We have to make a conscious effort to overcome this primal response.
—Sgt Q

Last chapter, I asked for that one memory you always push away. Let's not start with the biggest or worst one. Let's start with something small and try to reframe it. How do we take that hurt and turn it to hope? For me, it was reframing homelessness with building houses for the homeless—reframing negative deployments with a series of positive deployments across the globe to bring hope to the hopeless. It was reframing posttraumatic stress into this book to teach others.

After we've identified a memory, or a lion, as Mark Batterson calls it in his book *In a Pit with a Lion on a Snowy Day,* we will reframe it. You are going to practice it. You can know how to drive a car by reading a book and the owner's manual, but it's not until you get behind the wheel and hit the road that you'll become proficient and be issued a license to drive on the roads.

Whatever that hurt is, I am going to help build around you a positive neural network. If you were always criticized, then let me encourage you to focus on complimenting others, replacing the thoughts of criticism with memories of compliments. It's a lot easier to reframe thoughts when you can recall positive memories and emotions attached to them. Do this mental exercise in your head if you aren't yet comfortable speaking about it aloud.

Knowing and doing are very different. I require physical action to create new memories and experiences. That's exactly why I began building houses for the homeless in Mexico with YWAM (Youth with a Mission). That experience fostered Healing thru Service, and it has allowed me to create positive memories around my fear of homelessness.

With each experience, I create more positive memories from building homes in Mexico or performing outreach in Seattle and Auburn for the homeless community. I began to heal from my pain. Now I see the trauma of homelessness as a strength, not a weakness. I use that experience to connect with and encourage others who are homeless. I have fought the battle and won, so now I can empower others to do the same. I can truly help people in similar situations and make a lasting difference in their lives. If I had allowed the fear of homelessness to prevent me from acting, I would never have built fourteen-plus houses for homeless families or been able to help the veteran community. Building homes has created a positive neural network around that pain. This has taught me how to overcome the trauma of war with great success.

Enough about me. Let's explore how to reframe your thoughts.

Step 1. Write down that negative thought.

Step 2. Write down what you can find positive about this situation.

This may be difficult to do for two reasons. One, you may not have created any positive memories around this situation yet. Two, we all have a negative bias we have to fight. It is ingrained in us to focus on the negative aspect as a survival instinct. We have to make a conscious effort to overcome this primal response. You may think, *How can I find something positive from what has happened to me?* Here are three quick examples I can show you:

1. My dad was an abusive alcoholic, so I learned at a young age that I did not want to be like that with my own family. So now I

make it a point to drink very sparingly and raise my family differently.

2. My wife experienced tremendous abuse from her adopted family as a child. She could choose to live in that misery, or she could let go of that pain and use it to propel her into the life God has for her. She uses that energy not to be self-destructive, as so many of us do, but instead she uses it to help other women with similar experiences and has built a center for at-risk children in Cambodia.

3. I lost a good friend from high school and a fellow Marine during the War on Terror. I could continue to bury that memory with strong drink, or I could use it to propel me into helping other veterans overcome posttraumatic stress. My friend wouldn't have wanted me to drown his memory in a bottle of beer. He would want me to help others in memory of him because that's what he was doing when he died. He was helping others. He volunteered for his last mission so a Marine with a family could go on leave to visit his wife and kids. He was not just serving his country, but was serving his fellow Marine when he died. Things can be a mixture of both bad and good. We must choose what we focus on.

Step 3. Write down examples of what you can physically do to build positive memories.

I began, by accident, to build houses for the homeless. This act of compassion birthed from my pain was the greatest healing experience I had to overcome my fear of homelessness.

The build is on Memorial Day, and I use it as a quiet way to honor my friend each year. Now, with the creation of Operation Restore Hope, each build honors the memory of a fallen hero. We invite their family to be a part of the build. So often the family members of the fallen know how their loved one died, but very few of them know how they actually lived. So when they build with us, we are not only building a legacy for their family, but we are giving them a glimpse into the life of their loved one. Every person I take on mission to Mexico comes away with healing from something in their life. God has something for all of us here. Healing thru Service works. There is healing when you sacrifice for the betterment of others. That's just the way God designed it.

Step 4. How do I practice this on a regular basis?

I didn't just go once a year and build houses for the homeless and come away instantly cured. I wish that were the case, but the truth is that it's taken many years to get to this point in my life. Sorry, no quick fixes here—just diligent hard work. I went to Mexico once a year to build a home, but I'd also travel three or four more times a year around the globe building churches, schools, and orphanages with other groups. When stateside, I would serve in high school youth ministry and volunteer at my church and with other community outreach groups.

I didn't know at the time, but I was healing through serving others. I kept doing it. Every Sunday for four years I would be at my church at 8:00 a.m. to set up the chairs for service. I would then change over the chairs for the 11:00 a.m. and 12:30 p.m. services. I would even stay to remove all the chairs after the third service. I helped create the security team for the church and served on security each Sunday. We'd break for lunch around 2:00 p.m. and be back by 4:30 p.m. to begin cooking a meal for the high schoolers, who had their service in the evenings. I volunteered at all the kids and youth events and all the church outreaches. You get out what you put in. If you do this thing halfway, it will take you a lot longer to see results.

Step 5. Is there a way to practice this on a daily basis?

Try this: When something negative comes to mind, do not dwell on it. First and foremost, recognize it, and then shift your focus to the positive side of the issue. Here are some examples:

Stuck in traffic? Good. You may be avoiding an accident.

Didn't get the promotion? Good. More time to hone your current skills to become the subject matter expert.

Didn't get picked for the committee? Good. More time to focus on personal development.

If you begin to have an attitude of gratitude, you will see dramatic improvements in your mental state of mind and your personal relationships. Try to assume best intentions when someone rubs you the wrong way in a conversation. Learning these mental gymnastics will be a key to unlocking your true potential.

Debrief

We have a choice: allow our subconscious and sin nature to control our reactions, or use our conscious mind to retrain ourselves on the issue. Up to this point, every interaction I had regarding homelessness had been negative. Any time the word, thought, or conversation turned to the homeless, my subconscious would start pulling out all the files connected to it. The pain and anger would rise as well, which would be connected to Iraq, which was connected to . . . See the mental path of destruction? By making a conscious choice to go to Mexico and build that first house, I created a new neural pathway. I gave my mind a new memory to put in the homelessness file. I created hope, not just for the family receiving the house, but also in my mind.

It is hope, empowered by the Holy Spirit, that battles my posttraumatic stress.

Create hope files. Every home I build, every well I dig, every child's smile I see—they all add to that neural connection that creates hope files in every area of my life. These connections create a strong pathway in my brain. The subconscious is now under my control because I'm in control of the intel it gets on homelessness. It no longer brings up negative emotions; it brings up hope.

We can all do this with the difficult issues in our life. You don't need to leave the country to do this. You can do it right in your own home with your family. When something negative comes to mind, don't dwell on it. Instead, shift your focus to the positive side of the issue.

So, what is it for you? Were you discouraged as a child? You can reframe that hurt by making a conscious effort to encourage your own children, to encourage the children around you, or to encourage your friends. So often we repeat bad behavior we saw as a child. Find it too difficult? Pray to the Lord for the power and perseverance. We don't have to repeat it; we can reframe it.

Perhaps, like me, you wish you would have done more for your brothers-in-arms. We can't go back, but we can go forward and do more for them now. Volunteer with an NGO that helps veterans. Seek out others who are suffering and point them to resources like QMissions. The more you do this, the more positive experiences you will have, and the more hope files you will give your mind. Eventually, those negative panic files will be overflowing with hope, and the subconscious will not go into survival mode.

People always tell me, "I don't know what God has for me." I always tell them the same thing: "Find your pain, and there your ministry will be also." I again challenge you to "unlearn" the way you have been dealing with posttraumatic stress. Another good resource is *Man's Search for Meaning* by Viktor Frankl. It has been used at Wounded Warrior Battalion with great results.

CHAPTER 8

IDENTITY

*Our identity is how others will judge us and how we will
find our place in the world.*
—Sgt Q

Personal Recon

THE OTHER DAY I WAS LOOKING for a winter jacket in our hall closet.
As I dug past all the sweatshirts and parkas, I saw something I
hadn't seen in years—my Marine Corps dress blues. This iconic
uniform is renowned for its class and dignity and is easily identified around the world as being head-to-toe steeped in tradition.
It was a magnificent sight that brought back memories teeming
with emotion: the high collar, hearkening to the nickname "the

leathernecks" because of the bands of leather we'd wear around our necks to protect against sword strikes; the seven belt loops, each signifying one of the seven seas; the blue color representing our seafaring origin.

As I pulled it out, I looked it over carefully, studying the medals and stripes, each hard-fought for and won because of my military service. As I studied it, I couldn't help but notice how small it was. There is no way it would fit me now. It hadn't got smaller, but I had got bigger. Not just my chest and waist from gaining weight over the years, but because I had filled out. My shoulders had broadened, and my arms were bigger now. Looking at the uniform, I knew I was still a Marine, but I knew the uniform wouldn't fit me. I'd outgrown it. In the same way, the title of Marine didn't quite fit me anymore either. I had outgrown it. In fact, I'd grown so much as a man since the last time I'd worn that title that I couldn't fit into it any more than I could fit into those dress blues.

As humans, one of the most basic things we struggle with is our identity. Who are we? So often we find our identity in our affiliation. I am a Marine, a forward observer, a close combat instructor, and a master parachutist, but I am also a business owner, a father, a husband, and a missionary. I am a gun owner, a philanthropist, and an adventurer, but I am also a fighter of injustice and a lover of all things rare or unique. I am a wide-eyed vagabond of the Christ Follower Clan.

Am I the sum of all my parts, or something more? I am all things listed, but is that who I am? These are the questions we all at times pose to ourselves. Usually we reflect about this more when we have a major life change, such as separating from the military, changing careers, moving out of state, or seeing our children leave home. Any of these changes will cause us to search for and evaluate our identity.

Our identity is how we want to be known. Our identity is how others judge us and how we find our place in the world. Knowing who we are and claiming our identity is important to us. It gives us purpose and drives us to grow into maturity.

So many people struggle because they do not value or do not understand the value of their identity. It's a strange thing, identity. We all search for it not knowing what we're looking for. The very concept may be bubbling to the surface of your conscious mind for the first time as you contemplate who you are. Have you given it any serious thought? I'm willing to bet you've found your identity in the things you've done or in the job you're doing, but you haven't spent much time thinking about how your identity defines you and how you can shape it. Most people think identity is something thrust upon them because of an experience or position. What if I told you that your identity is in flux? What if I told you that you can make a conscious choice to change or improve it?

When I was in the Marines, I would spend a lot of time researching ancient battle tactics and warrior culture. I wanted to understand what made the greatest warriors so memorable that we still speak of them today. How could I learn from them—how could I become one of them? What I learned during those years not only helped me on the battlefield, but it helped me during my transition to civilian life.

Two of the most formidable groups of warriors on the battlefield were the Spartans and the Vikings. Despite their small numbers, they would easily outmaneuver and overpower the much larger armies of their opponents. In this chapter, I will focus on the superior battle tactics of the Spartans and Vikings and how we can apply them to our everyday battles.

Field Intel

The legacy of hardened warfighters also appeals to those
who wish to test their mettle and become one of the few
and the proud.
—Sgt Q

Do you know the meaning of the word *spartan*? The simple answer is it means "self-restrained," "simple," "frugal." The Spartans believed they were direct descendants of Hercules. It was this core belief that was the foundation of their warrior spirit. They believed it, and therefore trained like it. The culture revolved around loyalty to the state and military service. They had no veterans. They were considered to be in service from age seven to age seventy. They had a mindset and a "culture of war." They were full-time, all-the-time warriors. At the age of seven, the boys were indoctrinated into a military program known as the *agoge*.

Agoge emphasized duty, discipline, and endurance. The Spartans operated as one unit that considered no one soldier superior to another; they called themselves *homoioi*, or equal. The basis for their success was rooted in the belief of their lineage and their love for one another. Their fighting style, called the phalanx, illustrated this belief. The shield they carried was used not only to protect themselves, but to protect the man to the left. Their discipline, subjection to duty, and their comradery made them a superior fighting force on the battlefield—and they never left the battlefield.

Like the Spartans, the Vikings believed they were direct descendants of Odin and that when they died in battle, the Valkyries would come and carry them to Valhalla to feast for eternity with Odin.[36] When most people think of Vikings, they don't think of a well-organized fighting force. Hollywood conjures up Vikings as marauding, pillaging bands of raiders. They were those things, but they were also a well-disciplined, finely tuned fighting force. The Viking culture lived by nine common virtues, three of which were discipline, perseverance, and fidelity. Fidelity simply means faithfulness. Vikings were faithful at all costs. They protected one another and fought as one unit.

What can we learn from these two warrior cultures? Their identity, a structured belief in who they were, was fundamental

---

[36] https://englishhistory.net/vikings/viking-gods/.

to both the Spartans and the Vikings. I did not realize this at the time, but looking back I can see why the Marines focus on teaching the history of the Marine Corps so much in recruit training. They establish the foundation of a great warrior by creating an identity that is steeped in tradition to honor the warfighters who have come and gone. I believe this is one of the core reasons that we as Marines are so formidable on the battlefield. It is because we tell stories of the great warriors who came before us and how it is now our responsibility to honor and carry on that tradition of superior warfighting. We will fight harder and longer because we will not be the one to tarnish such a hallowed record.

The legacy of hardened warfighters also appeals to those who wish to test their mettle and become one of the few and the proud. I know because this is why I chose to join the Marines. I wanted to see if I had what it took to be counted as one of those acclaimed warfighters I'd heard about. Here I stand among the ranks of great men and women like Daniel Daley, Opha May Johnson, Carlos Hathcock, Lewis Burwell "Chesty" Puller, R. Lee Ermey, and Dakota Meyer. I am part of that storied tradition of warfighters, standing beside them and defending them at all costs. This idea of becoming a Marine, the ability to identify as one of the great warriors of our time, is what drives us to perform.

Take time to consider your identity—not who you were, but who you are now. What is your identity? Do you have a firm belief in your identity? What drives you to perform? Your identity, above all else, will affect the results of your performance.

Identity Research

Most can agree that the idea of an identity is important, but just how important is it really? Everyone at some point in their life will struggle with the concept of their own identity. Who am I?—the question posed by many over the span of human existence. The idea of self plays an important role in our mental health, and our life experiences shape our idea of self—how we see ourselves—our identity.

As much as our past experiences shape our idea of self, another powerful component is at play—our affiliations. Whom do we associate with? What groups do we self-identify with—a church, a club, or an organization? Many of us find our identity in our jobs and, more likely, our military service. This type of identity can be helpful as it creates a sense of belonging and comradery, a bond of shared view, and more importantly, a shared experience.

When we look at a shared experience and how it shapes identity, the first thing that comes to mind is my time in the Marines. As a Marine, I worked with other military branches, and now as the founder of QMissions, I not only work with the other branches, but also with many other civilian organizations. Not to knock the other branches of the military, but in my experience I have seen a vast difference between the comradery and pride in the Marines and that of the other branches of the military. The Marines seem to walk a little taller and talk a bit louder than the other branches. It isn't just that the Marines have a high opinion of themselves. Here is what others have to say about them:

> I have just returned from visiting the Marines at the front, and there is not a finer fighting organization in the world!
> —General of the Armies, Douglas MacArthur, Korea, September 21, 1950

> We have two companies of Marines running rampant all over the northern half of this island, and three Army regiments pinned down in the southwestern corner, doing nothing. What the hell is going on?
> —General John W. Vessey Jr., chairman of the Joint Chiefs of Staff during the assault on Grenada, 1983

The Marines I have seen around the world have the cleanest bodies, the filthiest minds, the highest morale, and the lowest morals of any group of animals I have ever seen. Thank God for the United States Marine Corps!
—Eleanor Roosevelt, first lady of the United States, 1945

Some people spend an entire lifetime wondering if they made a difference in this world. But, the Marines don't have that problem.
—Ronald Reagan, president of the United States, 1985

There are only two kinds of people that understand Marines: Marines and the enemy. Everyone else has a secondhand opinion.
—Genera William Thornson, US Army

I am convinced that there is no smarter, handier, or more adaptable body of troops in the world.
—Sir Winston Churchill, Prime Minister of Britain

The deadliest weapon in the world is a Marine and his rifle.
—General John "Black Jack" Pershing, US Army, commander of American forces in World War I[37]

In my experience, Marines are gung ho no matter what. They will all fight to the death. Every one of them just wants to get out there and kill. They are bad-ass, hard-charging mothers.
—Chris Kyle, *American Sniper: The Autobiography of the Most Lethal Sniper in US Military History*

[37] http://oldcorps.org/USMC/quotes.html.

But it isn't just our allies who hold the Marines in high regard. Here are some of the things our enemies have said about us. One of the most famous battles in Marine Corps history was the Battle of Belleau Wood. It is where the Marines would earn their most cherished nickname, the devil dogs.

On June 6, 1918, the Marines met face-to-face with the Germans in one of the most iconic battles in all of Marine Corps history. The Germans were dug in and heavily fortified in the tree line of Belleau Wood, protected by multiple machine gun emplacements and artillery. Within the first few days, the Marines suffered more than a thousand casualties. Undeterred, the Marines fought on trench by trench, foot by foot, clearing out the wooded area. They would fight for days without food and water, exhausted and wounded, but the Marines kept advancing their position, fighting hand to hand using anything within reach to best the enemy. For thirty days they pushed the Germans from the forest. The remaining Germans were completely terrified of the Marines' battle prowess.

> We got our nickname Devil Dogs from official German reports which called the Marines at Belleau Wood *Teufel Hunden*. It has been said that this nickname came about from Marines being ordered to take a hill occupied by German forces while wearing gas masks as a precaution against German mustard gas. While the Marines fought their way up the hill, the heat caused them to sweat profusely, foam at the mouth and turned their eyes bloodshot, and at some points the hill was so steep it caused the Marines to climb up it on all fours. From the Germans' vantage point, they witnessed a pack of tenacious, growling figures wearing gas masks, with bloodshot eyes and mouth foam seeping from the sides, advancing up the hill, sometimes on all fours, killing everything in their way. As the legend goes, the German

soldiers, upon seeing this spectacle, began to yell that they were being attacked by "dogs from hell."[38]

The stories of Marines and their fighting ability are not relegated to the distant past. Today's enemies have found out the hard way that the Marine Corps is a force to be reckoned with on the battlefield.

> When the Marines of 1st Battalion, 2nd Marines, did their first major clearing operation in the Musa Qala district, they intercepted a single Taliban transmission. That transmission was simple and to the point. It showed that the Taliban were not only taken aback by the Marines' violence of action, but absolutely terrified at the concept of having to fight these newcomers. The British were chickens. But these men . . . the American Marines . . . they fight like animals. Like they weren't even human. (Communications that were intercepted from a Taliban commander after they lost Karamanda to 1st Battalion, 2nd Marines—Funker530.com.)[39]

Friend or foe, the Marines are respected by all. They have earned their place among the most revered and feared warriors in history. Of all that has been said about the Marines—the leathernecks, the jarheads, the devil dogs—this quote by a chaplain says all that will ever need to be said about the Marine Corps: "You cannot exaggerate about the Marines. They are convinced to the point of arrogance, that they are the most ferocious fighters on earth—and

[38] Marines: The Official Website of the United States Marine Corps, "Belleau Wood," 1st Battalion History, https://www.6thmarines.marines.mil/Units/1st-Battalion/History/6thmarines.marines.mil/Units/1st-Battalion/History/.

[39] https://www.funker530.com/taliban-panda-ridge/?fbclid=IwAR21pgyxEcIw-b3IczdpYFdq0-LlkynhRjgT4rOOUwyT99A7QIhJ6BZDgZZ8.

the amusing thing about it is that they are" (Father Kevin Keaney, 1st Marine Division Chaplain, Korean War).[40]

The Marines are so formidable on the battlefield because we say we are, and then we prove it time and time again. From the day we stand on those yellow footprints and march into boot camp, we learn the history of the men who have come before us, the men of legend and reverence, the men whose legacy we stand on to meet the enemy on the field of battle.

When we graduate from boot camp and pin on our Eagle, Globe, and Anchor, we become part of this legacy, this brotherhood and fraternity of legendary warfighters. It is a title we never surrender. You may join the Army or the Navy, but you become a Marine. It is nothing less than this identity that will keep us in the fight long after what others thought was possible. It is the title of Marine and all its storied tradition that will not allow us to quit in the face of adversity.

As we explore this chapter on identity, I want you to take a serious look at your own identity and what aligns your self-image. Yes, I am still and always will be a Marine, but today I am so much more. I am a father and husband, a business owner and a leader. But most of all I am a man of God who chases after the lost sheep, rallying them to a new battle cry.

Scripture Unpack

If you were to remove one of the legs of a standard table, it will find balance, but once weight or pressure is applied, it will buckle and fall under the weight. Without the fourth leg, the table lacks the integrity to hold up to the stress of any additional weight.

—Sgt Q

The Spartans believed they were descendants of Hercules, and

---

[40] https://www.inc.com/bill-murphy-jr/happy-birthday-us-marine-corps-here-are-17-inspiring-quotes-about-marine-corps.html.

the Vikings believed they were descended from Odin. This fundamental belief was the foundation upon which their identities were built. So, from whom are we descended?

He who is in me is greater than he who is in the world (1 John 4:4). When we find our identity in Christ, we begin to see our value in the kingdom and transition into a kingdom mindset. We no longer chase frivolous things of the world, but instead we chase after God. Everything you may have learned in the military was not wasted. God was preparing you. He was preparing you for the next battlefield—the real one, the war between good and evil. He didn't design us to sit on the sidelines. He designed us for training and action, and we are now trained to fight His battle. We are no longer on the physical battlefield, but the spiritual one—or the mental battlefield, if you prefer that term. As we unpack this lesson, use your mind to draw similarities between the verses and your warrior mind, and let your mind be renewed with the things of God. Let's engage in some deeper training for this battle.

"That you put off, concerning your former conduct, the old man which grows corrupt according to the deceitful lusts, and be renewed in the spirit of your mind, and that you put on the new man which was created according to God, in true righteousness and holiness" (Ephesians 4:22–24 NKJV). You see, we are a new creation in Christ; therefore, our identity must be found in Him.

We must shed the old ways of thinking and assume the mind of Christ if we want to be victorious on this new battlefield. Other posttraumatic stress programs only address the physical, emotional, and mental sides of the trauma. They ignore the spiritual side. If you were to remove the leg of a standard table, it will find balance, but once you apply weight or pressure, it will buckle and fall under the weight. Without the fourth leg, the table lacks the integrity to hold up to the stress of any additional weight. Much is the same with other programs. If the spiritual side is not addressed and reinforced, is not healed and transformed, we will fail under added stress. We are spiritual beings; therefore, we must address this side of trauma if we seek to have any lasting results. Be renewed in the spirit of your mind. The MacArthur Study Bible explains it like this: "Salvation involves the mind (see Rom. 12:2; 2 Cor. 10:5), which is the center of thought, understanding and belief as well as motive and action (Col. 3:1–2, 10)."[41]

When a person becomes a Christian, God gives him a completely new moral and spiritual capability that a mind apart from Christ could never achieve. If we look further in Romans, we find four verses that illustrate how to have a God-centered mindset:

> For those who live according to the flesh set their minds on the things of the flesh, but those who live according to the Spirit, the things of the Spirit. For to be carnally minded is death, but to be spiritually minded is life and peace. Because the carnal mind is enmity against God; for it is not subject to the law of God, nor indeed can be. So then, those who are in the flesh cannot please God. (Romans 8:5–8 NKJV)

As warriors, we go farther than others think we can go, and we accomplish more than others think is possible. We have a unique ability to endure hardship and overcome insurmountable odds. How do we take our warrior attributes and apply them in our new life in Christ? How do we transition from one battlefield to the next? You see, it doesn't matter if we don't believe we are on the battlefield or not; we can't resist the reality of it. We can continue with our head down and take the hits, or we can wake up to the reality that we are standing on the battlefield of the mind. We can be a victim, or we can be victorious. There are no other options. We fight or die. Prepare for contact.

Let's take a closer look at how we put this into practice. What are some examples of self-serving thoughts vs. God-serving thoughts? It's as simple as changing the way we are phrasing the issue. Change

[41] John MacArthur, MacArthur Study Bible, ESV (Crossway, 2010), 386

your focus from the problem to the solution. What you focus on, you will find more of—right?

Change your thoughts from God—rescue me from this affliction, toward God—what are You trying to teach me in this trial?

Many of us want a new job because we're unhappy or we want more money so we can buy "X." What if we changed our prayer from asking for a new job to "Thanks for giving me this position that helps me to do my very best each day and gain favor with those around me," or "God refines me like silver so I can bring glory to the kingdom through the work of my hands"?

Changing the conversation we have with God will create a new man and void our old selfish desires. Be sure to come to God with a heart of thanksgiving and a request to glorify His name. Don't pray for your circumstances to change. Pray that you change to become stronger than your circumstances.

Create a new prayer life. Create a prayer to recite every day. Write it out. The prayer you are developing should be specific to your individual needs and place in the kingdom. It should be one of the first things you read in the morning and one of the last things you read before bed. I have mine taped to a mirror in my bathroom. I recite it as I brush my teeth. This way I start and end my day with a God-centered mindset. There is endless data to be found regarding self-affirmations and self-fulfilling prophecies. Let's change the narrative and speak God affirmations and God-fulfilling prophecies over our lives.

When I joined the Marines, I became a new person. I had to put away the childish things of my past and put on a new identity—that of a US Marine. There were certain standards and requirements for me, hundreds of years of tradition, and an esprit de corps I had to uphold. I was given a new uniform, a new mission, and a new way of life. There was no going back to who I was before. Ask anyone who knows a Marine before he enters boot camp and then sees him when he gets out. They will tell you he is not the same person. He has changed on a fundamental level. He walks a bit taller and looks a bit sharper. They can't quite put their finger on it, but they can tell you that there is something different about them. When we decide to follow Christ, He, too, gives us a new identity and a new mission. Consider these verses: "Your word have I hid in my heart, that I might not sin against you" (Psalm 119:11 KJV 2000), and "And be renewed in the spirit of your mind" (Ephesians 4:23 KJV 2000).

Write down the lies you tell yourself. What are the things in your head that are dragging you down? Now study Scripture to combat each one of those lies. I do this by searching for the keywords in my statement and seeing what the Bible says about those words and concepts.

Each Scripture of truth is a weapon to use against the enemy, but what good is a weapon if you don't use it, train with it, or depend on it? Take a tank for example. An M16 won't damage it. You need a better weapon to defeat it. If you've acquired a TOW missile and have been trained to use it, when that tank enters your AO, you'll be able to defeat it. Scripture can be used in the same way. The Bible calls the Word of God a sword, a weapon of war. It's time to pick up your weapon and take the fight to the enemy.

Ask yourself, *Who do I want to be? An angry, heartbroken shell of my former self?* I wasted many good years of my life waiting for a hero to come and save me. I wanted someone to take away the pain, to fix all my problems, to make all my symptoms go away, and so on. I was looking for a worldly savior, some rich uncle or something like that. Well, that earthly hero never showed up.

Instead, Jesus Christ saved me from my sins, my spiritual blindness, and my lostness. The Lord set at my feet a new suit of armor with new weapons of war. He then told me to get to work. Did He snap His fingers, and suddenly all my problems vanished? No, all those things that were burdening me before were still there. But He taught me a new way and gave me His power. I had to learn to look past my troubles and on to what God had for me. I still face adversity, but I am well disciplined and do not flinch in the face of the enemy.

All those things that held me back and all those things I thought I needed to overcome before I moved forward didn't fade away. I had to decide to face them head-on. Only when I decided to help others did my healing start. When I agreed to go to Mexico that first time and build a house for a homeless family, that was the first time I felt relief from my symptoms and received the reward of joy in the work I was doing.

Ask yourself:

> Who do I want to be?
>
> Do I want to be angry, full of self-loathing, broken? Or do I want to be a hero again?
>
> Do I have what it takes to rise from the ashes of battle, war-torn and beaten, and put on the full armor of God?
>
> Do I have what it takes to train my mind in the ways of the Lord and join Jesus on the spiritual battle-field—a battle for the souls of my brothers and sisters?
>
> Do I lie down and die, or do I stand up and fight?
>
> Will I lie down among the memories of the dead, or will I rise from the ashes like the phoenix and set the world on fire with the love of God?

Tactical Application

Developing your identity can seem like a daunting task, but the following five steps have helped me find out who I am and have helped me develop into the person I wanted to become. Each year, I spend time learning a new skill or developing one that is lacking. Last year, it was to become a public speaker. This year, it's to become a better encourager of my friends and family. Regardless of what I choose, each year these five areas are always in a constant state of improvement.

1. Read More

Since beginning this journey, I've read countless medical journals and research studies regarding the brain, how it operates, and its connection to the body. I have not just read psychology magazines and scientific journals, but writings by Bible scholars—and of course, there's my never-ending study of the Bible. I watch very little sports on TV, opting instead to spend my time learning new concepts. At times, I feel like I am filled with useless facts.

2. Pray More

The power of prayer will do more for you than you think. It is your direct link to the Creator and is part of the fundamental process of rewiring your brain. Casting your burdens upon God and allowing yourself the comfort of knowing you don't have to fix everything yourself will bring a peace beyond understanding. Pray for things of the kingdom and for the ability and mental fortitude to withstand the furnace of affliction.

3. Serve

Serving has helped me more than any single action I have ever taken. Serving others will without a doubt bring healing to your soul. Through service to others, I have found my purpose and have taught many others to do the same. The joy of unselfishly giving your time and investing in something bigger than yourself is rewarding and has become the motto for my life: Healing thru Service. It works.

4. Find a Mentor

We all need people we can trust in our lives, people who can speak life into us and give us gentle correction. It may seem scary at first to allow yourself to be held accountable by another person, but as iron sharpens iron, one brother sharpens another. A fresh perspective is valuable because most of the time our ability to appropriately self-evaluate is severely lacking.

5. Invest

Invest in others. Become someone's biggest cheerleader. This does not mean you have to fix all their problems or tell them how to fix them. It means to genuinely lift others up and encourage them in their daily walk. When you seek to build others up, your influence will grow tremendously, and you will gain the respect of your peers without even trying.

Ask yourself, *How I can improve in these five areas?* Later, I will reference how to use the SRD (Structure, Routine, Discipline) process and apply the C + T = S (Consistency + Time = Success) formula. Watch what happens.

Debrief

After I left the Marines, I struggled. I longed to go back—back to the identity I once had. I couldn't; I had outgrown it. Since then, I have become bigger and better than I once was, and now I cannot fit back into the shell of that person. It would be like a lobster trying to squeeze back into its old shell. Did you know that lobsters shed their shells as they grow? I didn't either. What Rabbi Abraham Twerski shares with us in this passage will dramatically shed some light on our identity and how we can grow uncomfortable inside our former identity:

> The lobster's a soft mushy animal that lives inside of a rigid shell. That rigid shell does not expand. Well, how can the lobster grow? Well, as the lobster grows, that shell becomes very confining, and the lobster feels itself under pressure and uncomfortable. It goes under a rock formation to protect itself from predatory fish, casts off the shell, and produces a new one. Well, eventually, that shell becomes very uncomfortable as it grows. Back under the rocks. The lobster repeats this numerous times.

The stimulus for the lobster to be able to grow is that it feels uncomfortable. Now, if lobsters had doctors, they would never grow because as soon as the lobster feels uncomfortable, goes to the doctor, gets a Valium, gets a Percocet, feels fine, never casts off his shell. I think that we have to realize that times of stress are also times that are signals for growth, and if we use adversity properly, we can grow through adversity.[42]

Finding your identity in things of this world is futile. They don't last. They change or deteriorate. You become unable to be what you once were. Many professional athletes suffer with this very thing, trying to find out who they are after their sport has surpassed their physical capabilities. I could find my own identity in many of my accomplishments. Those things are fleeting, and they just don't last. I'm too old and broken to perform as the Marine I once was. The market could change, and my business could fail. Then who would I be? No; instead, I choose to find my identity in God and in the love He has for me.

I'm a child of God and now a warrior for Him. I have taken up the Great Commission as my mantle, and it is there that I find my identity. Your identity in Christ is the only place you can put your trust and never have it broken. Man will fail us, but God never will. We can all find our identity in Christ, but the Christian warrior lifestyle is not a part-time affair. You do not try to be a warrior; you either are one or you aren't. It's the same for integrity; you either have integrity or you don't. For the warrior, falling short of a goal does not signify failing. Quitting does. Falling short just means you will try harder next time.

"Do or do not—there is no try" (Yoda).

---

[42] Rory Stirling, "The Rabbi and the Lobster," Greater Good in Action, August 17, 2017, https://ggia.berkeley.edu/practice/practice_as_pdf/finding_silver_linings?printPractice=Y.

CHAPTER 9

KNOW YOUR ENEMY

*Understanding the enemy in your mind can create a
better battle plan for your life.*
—Sgt Q

Personal Recon

I REMEMBER SITTING ON THE PLANE headed to Iraq. Most people were
sleeping, telling jokes, or playing grab-ass as we flew toward what
would be, for most of us, our first real battle. Instead, I was reading
over old battle plans and intel reports from the First Gulf War in
the mid-1990s. This was a new war, but it was against a common
enemy. I knew there would be valuable information to gather from
the experience of others who had come and fought before. I was

especially interested in how they might counter our air superiority and robust indirect fire capabilities. I needed to understand the history of their tactics so I could avoid their countermeasures. As a forward observer on the battlefield, I needed to make sure I would be effective and formidable. I also knew that the more I understood their countermeasures, the better I could keep our pilots and ground forces safe while sending devastating ordnance to disrupt enemy movement. Two things stood out to me during my research.

In an Iraqi Army artillery manual, I found a tactic for countering our aircraft. They would aim their artillery to the sky and fire barrages of shells with airburst fuses in attempts to hit our aircraft with the shrapnel of the blast. Not a very effective anti-air tactic, but I am sure it would scare the hell out of a pilot to have hundreds of rounds banging around him. I learned two things. One, treat all artillery as anti-air and avoid sending aircraft near those positions. Two, if I did send aircraft to hit artillery positions, use fast movers that would be well out of range by the time they got rounds in the air.

The second interesting bit of intel I discovered was how they would use tanks to counter our tanks and avoid our indirect fire. They would dig giant sloped holes in the sand and back the tanks in. This essentially created parking spots for the tanks below ground level. They would dig them deep enough to hide a tank, but not so deep that the main gun was under the sand. They would leave just the main gun exposed. This way they could fire on our advancing ground forces without fear of taking any direct hits because the bodies of their tanks would be underground. This also protected them from indirect fire such as artillery and mortars. We would have to score direct hits to inflict any damage. A near miss would only send shrapnel over their heads. The slope and reverse parking would also allow for a quick getaway if they were overrun.

I learned two things from this tactic: One, HEPD (High Explosive Point Detonating) rounds, which are standard for this type of engagement, would be ineffective. So we would need to switch to DPICM (Dual-Purpose Improved Conventional Munition) and WP (White Phosphorus) rounds for the dug-in tanks. The WP is a chemical burning agent that, with an airburst, settles over the tanks and affects any exposed ground troops. It instantly raises the internal temperature of the tanks, making it unbearable for the tank crew. It turns their tank into an Easy-Bake Oven. (Special note: the use of WP against troops in the open is not banned by Geneva conventions or by our Rules of Engagement, but it is still highly controversial. However, using it against equipment and armored vehicles is not specifically mentioned in any of the UN General Assembly notes that I could find.)

I knew I needed to learn as much about my enemy and their tactics as I could to ensure the safety and survival of my fellow warfighters. In the same way, understanding the enemy in your mind can help you create a better battle plan for your life and increase your personal survival and the survival of your relationships.

Field Intel

Overwhelming us to the point of suicide.
—Sgt Q

In combat, it is normal to study the enemy's history and tactics. We seek to uncover their strengths so we can avoid them, and we seek to learn their weaknesses so we can exploit them. I, like many others in the military, spent a good deal of my time reading intel reports to gain access to this vital information.

Living a life with posttraumatic stress is no different. We must study our enemy so we can learn the strengths and weaknesses. This way we can be victorious and live a full and rewarding life. I think what we all want is peace in our heart and control over our mind. In this chapter, we will discuss how to identify an enemy and how to use our military mind to defeat it. For each of us, the enemy will be different, but the tactics we use will be the same. Posttraumatic stress can include a multitude of symptoms, each more complex than the next, but they all have the same goal. They want what every enemy wants—to kill us.

Posttraumatic stress uses standard ambush techniques. During an ambush, the enemy uses the element of surprise to gain the advantage. The enemy wants to separate you from your squad. Once separated, they can pin you down with intersecting fields of fire. Then, they overwhelm and kill you. Isn't that what posttraumatic stress does to us? Doesn't it feel like an ambush when we are hit with a sudden panic attack? We are usually caught off guard, and the anxiety causes us to isolate from friends and family. The negative and intrusive thoughts continue to bombard our minds, mentally pinning us down, overwhelming us to the point of suicide.

Go ahead, read that again slowly. Have you never correlated the two scenarios? Something fundamental is changing in your mind. You realize posttraumatic stress is an enemy like any other, and it can be defeated. As we begin to shift to our tactical mind, we will become acutely aware of the tactics we learned in the military and how to employ them to be victorious.

Ambush techniques are not new to the battlefield. They have been used successfully in every major conflict on record. One of the most effective ambushes actually changed the course of history by stopping the superior Roman legion from its conquest of Germany's nomadic tribesmen. Peter S. Wells, author of *The Battle That Stopped Rome*, states:

> It was one of the most devastating defeats ever suffered by the Roman Army, and its consequences were the most far-reaching. The battle led to the creation of a militarized frontier in the middle of Europe that endured for 400 years, and it created a boundary between Germanic

and Latin cultures that lasted 2,000 years.[43]

In September of AD 9, the Roman legate Publius Quincti-
lius Varus set out confidently with an estimated 15,000 seasoned
legionnaires from their summer quarters on the Weser River, an
area now known as northwestern Germany. His army headed west
toward permanent bases near the Rhine. They were planning to
investigate reports of an uprising among local tribes and to quell
any disturbance.

Varus, fifty-five, was linked by marriage to the imperial family
and had served as Emperor Augustus's representative in the prov-
ince of Syria (which includes modern Lebanon and Israel), where
he had been previously successful at putting down ethnic distur-
bances. As they marched farther and farther from their support,
they became easy targets. The nearest Roman base lay at Haltern,
sixty miles to the southwest, yet Varus pressed on. On the third
day, he and his troops entered a passage between a hill and a huge
swamp known as the Great Bog, which was no wider than sixty feet
in places. It was here that wave upon wave of nomadic tribesmen
rushed the ranks of the advancing Roman army using what are now
classic ambush tactics—hitting hard and fast, cutting lines through
the ranks and isolating individual soldiers, killing them, and then
running away to regroup in the thick woods, only to rush again
from another direction.

As the increasingly chaotic and panicky mass of legionnaires,
cavalrymen, mules, and carts inched forward, Germans appeared
from behind trees and sand-mound barriers, cutting off all possibility of retreat. The story continues:

> In open country, the superbly drilled and disciplined
> Romans would surely have prevailed. . . . But here,

---

[43] Fergus M. Bordewich, "The Ambush That Changed History," *Smithsonian.*
com, Smithsonian Institution, September 1, 2006, www.smithsonianmag.com/
history/the-ambush-that-changed-history-72636736/.

with no room to maneuver, exhausted after days of hit-and-run attacks, unnerved, they were at a crippling disadvantage.[44]

Varus understood there was no escape. Rather than face certain torture at the hands of the Germans, he chose suicide, falling on his sword as the Roman tradition prescribed. Most of his commanders followed suit, leaving their troops leaderless in what had become a killing field.

An army unexcelled in bravery, the first of Roman armies in discipline, in energy, and in experience in the field, through the negligence of its general, the perfidy of the enemy, and the unkindness of fortune . . . was exterminated almost to a man by the very enemy whom it has always slaughtered like cattle," according to the AD 30 account of Velleius Paterculus, a retired military officer who may have known both Varus and Arminius.[45]

Sometimes we feel this way, don't we? We are hit by wave upon wave of panic and disturbing thoughts that give way to nightmares and anger, further destroying out mental sanctity. These relentless attacks isolate us from our family, our friends, and our squad. Left alone, exhausted, and hopeless, many choose to end their lives as Varus did, by taking his own life rather than experience torture. There are many enemies we will face with the adversary, posttraumatic stress. I have provided a short list of posttraumatic stress strengths and weaknesses.

- Strengths of posttraumatic stress: alcohol, drugs, isolation, anger, unforgiveness, selfishness, self-loathing, apathy, and

[44] Bordewich, "The Ambush That Changed History."
[45] Bordewich, "The Ambush That Changed History."

the most dangerous of all, the submission to a victim mentality

- Weaknesses of posttraumatic stress: sober-minded, community, joy, forgiveness, serving, positive self-talk, empathy, and empowerment

This is not an exhaustive list, but it includes common traits most of us can relate to. Whatever your enemy looks like, the employment of SRD (Structure, Routine, and Discipline) and SMC (Shoot, Move, and Communicate) will assure victory. You cannot simply be an observer of your life; you must be an active participant in your healing. You need to train in these tactics and use them daily so when the attack does occur, you will be ready to quickly identify and defeat them. These are techniques I have used with success for many years, and I have successfully taught others to employ the same tactics to achieve victory.

Scripture Unpack

> *Whatever evil thing you cut out of your life, it is*
> *important to add back in something honorable.*
> —Sgt Q

As Christians, we see the enemy not just as the personal combatant in our minds, but as a global enemy against the church. Satan and his army seek to isolate each of us from the church and the body of believers. "We do not wrestle against flesh and blood, but against principalities, against powers, against the rulers of the darkness of this age, against spiritual hosts of wickedness in the heavenly places" (Ephesians 6:12 NKJV).

I am afraid that those who choose to dismiss the Scripture in this book, who choose to forgo fighting on the spiritual battlefield, will have limited success in their fight against posttraumatic stress.

For the rest of you, these Scripture Unpack sessions will give you the leading edge and will tip the scales of battle in the war that wages in your mind. Accepting salvation and inviting the Holy Spirit into your life will give you a deeper understanding of these universal truths. Having this connection with God through the sacrifice of Jesus Christ is like adding cream to your coffee: once combined, they cannot be separated.

These battles we wage in our minds, these addictions of anger and regret, are all ambush tactics of the enemy to keep you from completing the mission God has for you. Don't worry if you don't know what that mission is yet. I didn't realize mine for many years. I warn you not to focus on the work God has for you, but rather focus on the God who has sent you to work.

The closer you are to God, the more He will reveal to you. In the book *Jesus Was an Airborne Ranger*, the author, a chaplain for a Ranger battalion, reminds us that our enemy is not people or policies, but evil spirits in heavenly places.[46] The evil of people and policies is the direct result of spiritual influences. If we want to win the war, then we must take the battle into enemy territory. We must fight on a spiritual battlefield; otherwise, we will continue to fight the same battles. We need to take the strongholds the enemy has in our lives, and we must look past our symptoms and into the cause. The spiritual war is where we are called to fight.

How do we begin? Well, Jesus Christ has already won the victory for us on the cross. So, what is your part? How much do you want victory? A good way to start is by drawing near to the Lord through humble prayer, fasting, and studying the Bible. Learn about the full armor of God in Ephesians 6:10–18. Look to Him for your power and wisdom, and He will guide you.

If we want victory, we must be willing to sacrifice and yield to Him—sacrifice our time and our money for healing. We need to give up the things we know are not healthy for us. We also need to turn from our old ways that bring us pain and become a new

[46] John McDougall, *Jesus Was an Airborne Ranger: Finding Your Purpose Following the Warrior Christ*, Multnomah Books, 2015.

creation by the renewing of our mind. Know that the enemy will try to whisper lies in your ears and remind you of all the wrong you have done. Don't listen to him. He will tempt you with drugs, alcohol, sex, destructive relationships—the list goes on and on. You must cut out those things in your life that do not honor God. I don't need to take time to list them all, to explain, or to justify your behavior. You, and you alone, know the things in your life God is calling you to turn from. What is sin for one may not be sin for another, so be mindful not to put your yoke on someone else.

Ask God what areas He wants you to change, and He will convict your heart of those things. Turn from them and be set free. Something honorable must replace whatever evil thing is cut out of your life. If you don't replace a destructive behavior with a positive one, you'll create a hole in your life that will become a trap you'll be sure to fall back into—the very thing we want to avoid. Matthew 12:43–45 (author's paraphrase) illustrates this quite well: "If an unclean spirit leaves a man, but that man doesn't replace it with something better, that spirit will return and bring seven worse than itself with it." Take some time to study on this before moving on to the tactical application.

Prayer, meditation, and healing: I've debated where to add this gem of my experience and how to present it to you, and I've decided to settle it here. During my time studying the brain, more than one study and medical journal led me to the unpacking of meditation and how it relates to healing our mind. Meditation is mentioned multiple times in the Bible, especially in the book of Psalms. We're told repeatedly to meditate on the Word of God. So how do we do this? What is the difference between what the world calls meditation and what we call prayer? Let's break this area down to avoid confusion.

Prayer. We all know, or think we know, what prayer is—talking to God. Jesus talked to God. He drew alone to pray. There are lots of ways to pray. We can pray by ourselves or in a group (Acts 2:42), make prayers of request and intercession (1 Timothy 2:1), or offer prayers of thanksgiving (Psalm 95:2–3). And we can pray in the Spirit (1 Corinthians 14:14–15).

Meditation. Biblical meditation is different; it's focusing on the *truth* of the Word of God (Psalm 119:15, 27, Psalm 143:5, and John 14:24 talk about that). We can also go a step further and use our imagination to help focus our thinking and make biblical scenes more vivid. Scripture doesn't forbid using an image in the imagination to help focus upon the Lord. It's called *visualization*, and it's part of the gift God has given us in our imagination. Problems can arise when we think the image we make becomes or is inhabited by the Holy Spirit at our beck and call—that's trying to control God through a created image and is a form of idolatry (Exodus 20:4). That's when we have the potential to step into the area of occult visualization and can begin to use power from the dark side. And that is very dangerous.

The Bible warns against false visions created by our own minds (Ezekiel 13, especially v. 17; Jeremiah 23:16–18). It frequently points out how untrustworthy and wicked our imagination is and condemns those using it for their own purposes. Scripture says we may have what we ask for only when we ask in God's will (1 John 5:14–15).

Many may argue that meditation and prayer are at odds with each other because of the confusion arising from the widespread use of such occult methods through the spread of the New Age movement, but I'm here to tell you they don't have to be at odds. Both are part of a healthy prayer life. What is the intent behind your meditation? Worldly meditation is self-centered, and prayerful meditation is God-centered and directed by the Holy Spirit and God's Word. Guard your heart.

According to a report on NBC News, there's a direct link between prayer, meditation, and healing. The link between deep reflection and a decrease in action can be a useful one when dealing with a trauma or other negative situations. Dr. Paul Hokemeyer, a marriage, family, and addictions therapist, says:

Prayer and meditation are highly effective in lowering our reactivity to traumatic and negative events. They are powerful because they focus our thoughts on something outside ourselves. During times of stress, our limbic system, more commonly known as our central nervous system, becomes hyper-activated, which does two things: it thrusts us into survival mode where we freeze, fight or flee the situation, [such that] we move away from the present state of being into a future state. This also shuts down our executive functioning [and] prevents us from thinking clearly. This is why when we're stressed out we can make poor decisions and act in self-destructive ways.[47]

When scientists studied the brain-scanned images of those meditating and those deep in prayer, they were astounded to find that the images matched. The exact same areas of the brain lit up in both those meditating and those in prayer. The remarkable results left them with more questions than answers.

However you pray or meditate, make it in reverence to the Lord. Unsure? Need further proof? In the back of the book, I have laid out some Scriptures so that you can practice this art of meditating on God's Word. Study the verses and meditate on them.

Here's another exercise that helps me. I believe it's better placed here in the Scripture section than in the practical application because this is truly a spiritual exercise. I do this exercise with reverence to the Lord, for He has given this gift to me, and to give me comfort when my mind is troubled and the battle wages around me. I've tried all sorts of meditation and visualization techniques over the course of many years, but peace only comes through meditating on the Word of God. Through trial and error, and many

[47] Nicole Spector, "This Is Your Brain on Prayer and Meditation," *NBCNews. com*, NBCUniversal News Group, February 16, 2018, www.nbcnews.com/better/health/your-brain-prayer-meditation-ncna812376.

sleepless nights, I was finally able to quiet my mind in the midst of battle and find rest. Sleep was always most difficult for me after returning from Iraq. With this simple technique, I have regained control of my mind as I put it to rest.

I use this when my brain just won't quiet down and when it wants to think of anything and everything as I'm trying to fall asleep. I call it my rule of seven, and it works like this:

Prayer: *Father God, focus my mind on you and bring my mind under submission to Your will.*

- Slowly inhale for a count of seven: 1 . . . 2 . . . 3 . . . 4 . . . 5 . . . 6 . . . 7
- Hold your breath for a count of seven: 1 . . . 2 . . . 3 . . . 4 . . . 5 . . . 6 . . . 7
- Breathe out quickly for a count of seven: 1 . . . 2 . . . 3 . . . 4 . . . 5 . . . 6 . . . 7 (at 5, 6, 7, there is no air in my lungs)

I do this as many times as necessary. I keep focused on my breathing and do not entertain any other thoughts running around in my mind. Breathe slowly and rhythmically. Do not hurry your count, but keep an even pace. It may feel awkward at first, but with practice you will succeed. For me, this is my time to seek refuge in the Lord.

Tactical Application

Since we can now look at posttraumatic stress as the enemy and a panic or anxiety attack as an enemy ambush, we can also adapt military techniques to defeat them.
—Sgt Q

If you haven't noticed, each chapter has built upon another. You've built things you didn't fully understand. I have, in a way, "Mr. Miyagied" you.

Now is the time to start putting it all together—to start forming those weapons of warfare. I do not have to reinvent the wheel here. We take the things we already know and repurpose them from battling a physical enemy to battling the enemy in our mind—posttraumatic stress. It is easier for me to see the battlefield in my mind as a physical one and to employ similar tactics to become victorious.

We all have those sudden panic attacks or feelings of uneasiness. Recognizing the signs and sensations in your body so you can battle the panic before it reaches full strength is critical. For me, I can feel the stress hormones coursing through my veins. I know when I need to start talking myself down, and fast.

Think back to your training. What did the military teach you to do when you encountered the enemy? When you're pinned down in a firefight or caught in an ambush, what do you do? Stay there? No! Shoot, move, and communicate. You return fire to push the enemy back, maneuver to get out of the kill zone, and call reinforcements. You fight. Your internal conflicts are no different. You must fight them with the same maneuvers and vigor as you would a physical enemy.

Let's take some time to review what we've learned and form it into something we can use.

1. Understanding the brain: the negative bias memory you wrote down
2. Overcoming the negative bias: reframing the memory to find the positive aspect
3. Controlling the subconscious: using the grounding technique to overcome the amygdala hijack
4. Listening to your body: recognizing triggers in your environment

Next up: Going into battle: SMC (Shoot, Move, Communicate) basics.

This is a squad technique I learned in 1st ANGLICO. We were

a small group of forward observers and communication specialists whose primary function on the battlefield was to call on fire to suppress the enemy for an infantry assault or to rain devastation artillery and close air support on dug-in enemy positions. Once in place, our use of cover and concealment in the OP would keep us protected and out of the enemy's crosshairs.

Our most vulnerable time was when we were on patrol to our OP and back to the main body of the supporting element. For this reason, we trained extensively on how to avoid a small arms engagement and ambushes. With a small team of six to eight men, we would easily be outmatched in a firefight with any other unit on the battlefield. We carried no heavy machine guns or rockets of any kind, opting instead for multiple man-packed radio systems, GPS, and extra batteries. As an ANGLICO team, our strength did not come from direct action engagements, but from our superior naval gunfire, airpower, artillery, and mortars. We would rehearse several techniques for escaping an ambush, as our small-sized element would be quickly overrun in a straight-up small arms engagement. My favorite maneuver was called the Australian Peel. It was designed to put the greatest possible distance between you and the enemies' kill zone. The center of every technique was a simple framework—Shoot, Move, Communicate (SMC)—and there were three main components:

Shoot: If compromised, we would immediately return fire with the volume and consistency of a much larger element. This was to put the enemy on their heels and make them pause for a moment to consider who the hell they just picked a fight with.

Move: We would listen, then quickly move in the direction specified by the commander. We would move in a bounding formation, with all but one man laying down cover as a single soldier egressed from the kill zone. The next man in the formation would follow his path, stopping only after he passed the last man. He would then turn and begin returning fire until it was his time to peel out again. A well-organized team could move the distance of a football field in under a minute. We all knew that if we stopped moving, we would surely be pinned down and die. Stay on the move and stay alive.

Communicate: This is a key element in any military operation, but none more so than when you are in an ambush. Relaying your position allows others to know you are in distress, and nearby units can render assistance. For us, there usually were not any other friendlies in the AO. The best we could hope for was to relay our current position to fire direction control (FDC) and move quickly out of the area as we called fire in on our last location.

SMC is a risky move, but it illustrates the importance of moving out of the kill zone. That's because you know an operator is already on the hook relaying the grid, and that in a few minutes there will be a heavy volume of ordnance inbound on that position. Since we can now look at posttraumatic stress as the enemy and a panic or anxiety attack as an enemy ambush, we can also adapt military techniques to defeat them.

Shoot: Return fire. Speak truth.

When you feel panic, remind yourself where you are and that you're safe. If you feel depressed, remind yourself you are loved by God, by family, and by us, your brothers-in-arms. If you feel regret, remind yourself you are forgiven and that you have been washed clean through Jesus Christ. Combat the lies with biblical truth. Change the conversation in your mind.

Move: Maneuver. Change your mindset.

Remove self-loathing. Continue to speak biblical truth until your mind becomes renewed. Some days may be more difficult than others. Romans 12:2 (NIV) says, "Do not conform to the pattern of this world, but be transformed by the renewing of your mind. Then you will be able to test and approve what God's will is—his good, pleasing and perfect will."

Communicate: Communicate. Call in reinforcements.

Call your battle buddy, call your spouse, call your pastor, call someone. It doesn't matter who you call, but make sure to call somebody. Express how you feel. Pray together.

I will walk onto the battlefield with any one of you, day or night. Don't feel embarrassed. The feeling of embarrassment is the enemy. Would you be embarrassed to call for help during an ambush? I'm betting not. How is this situation any different? It's also good to communicate with others about your triggers so people don't inadvertently push them. Walk through those emotions with them so you both will gain a better understanding.

You will also need to develop your own personal SMC—something that resonates with you, words that have value to you. Each one of us will create something different, unique to our personal journey, but the results will be the same. After much practice, your mind will be disciplined to take back control of your emotions. A simple SMC may look like this:

S: Repeat "I am safe. I am loved. I am valued."

Tell yourself where you are right now and who you are. Note the exits, stay safe, stay in control.

M: Repeat "I am in control. I direct my thoughts. I choose my actions."

Stay here as long as needed or as long as you need. You can move calmly away from the trigger, either physically or mentally, at a time of your choosing. You are in control.

C: Repeat "I am well-trained and victorious. I know to call for help when ambushed."

Tell the people you are with the discomfort you are feeling. Call your spouse or battle buddy. When you speak these things out, it takes the power away.

Debrief

Creating a correct mindset, studying your enemy, and having a battle plan before you're engaged is a valuable tactic in the battle of posttraumatic stress. Over the years, I've developed the tools of warfare. These tools are the weapons I fight with on the battlefield of my mind as the enemy threatens to ravage my body and make me physically ill.

The hardest part of this will be the communication part. Having the wherewithal to tell others you are suffering will be a hurdle for most. It is still hard for me at times to admit I am struggling. After all, I am the subject matter expert, right? I've received many accolades and awards for my work in the field of posttraumatic stress and healing. All the lessons in this book are for me as well as for you. Success can be a stumbling block because it prevents us from being honest and vulnerable with others. Remember these lessons.

The darkness and the light cannot occupy the same space. Light casts no shadow, so whatever is in the darkness when you bring it to light must flee. What does this mean? Our struggles are the darkness, and if we bring them to the light—tell others we are struggling—the darkness must flee because it cannot occupy the same space. Darkness is an illusion; it does not exist. Darkness is not the opposite of light; darkness is merely the absence of light.

Journaling has helped me quite a bit. Journaling will help you too. It will help you express the thoughts swirling around in your head. More importantly, it will help you track your progress and show you how far you've come and how much ground you've taken back from the enemy. It has helped me write this book and pass the hard-learned knowledge on to you. My hope is that it will give you the upper hand in the battle you wage in your body and in your mind. I've included an excerpt from my personal journal in the back of the book as an example.

Everything in this book has led to this point. I could have easily just started with these techniques, but without understanding how they were created, I would have failed by not educating you. From this part forward, I will begin to unpack all the things God has revealed to me while on the mission field serving His people. It has not been easy, and I have experienced a lot of trials along the way. So you, too, will face adversity, but hopefully our time together will leave you better prepared to meet the challenges ahead.

Battling the effects of war is mind over matter. It's about not being a victim of your circumstances. In the next chapter, we will talk about creating structure with the renewing of your mind. Consistency forms structure, which is half the formula to success, and building a routine reinforces the mindset we hope to create. And the most important part is discipline. I know that is a nasty word we all think we know, but do we really? Can we say we are disciplined in our workout, job, loving our spouse, and in our mind? In our walk with God? Don't worry; it's all going to come together.

CHAPTER 10

SRD:

Structure, Routine, Discipline

*The more you sweat in training, the less you will
bleed in battle.*
—Sgt Q

Personal Recon

IN THE MARINES, WE HAD TO do physical fitness tests every quarter.
Everyone dreaded it, but we all did it. These tests would consist of a
three-mile run followed by sit-ups and pull-ups. Each exercise was
worth 100 points, and you wanted to max out each one to get a
total of 300. This point system was not just about bragging rights;

it could have a huge impact on your military career and opportunities within the unit. The higher the score, the better ranking you received to be considered for additional schooling. The higher the points, the better your promotion score and the faster you were promoted. The better the performance, the better the chance you would go up on a meritorious promotion board or receive a nomination for NCO (noncommissioned officer) of the quarter. These three exercises weigh heavily on the career of a Marine. To max out on the run, you had to do it in under eighteen minutes. To max on the sit-ups requires 100 in two minutes, and the pull-ups are twenty without getting off the bar. Pull-ups is where most guys lose points. Now, most in the Marines are big, but I was not. I weighed in at 125 pounds, standing five-foot-four. That's about the size of your average freshman high schooler. So I excelled at the pull-ups. It's much easier to lift 125 pounds than 225. For this reason, my promotion score was always really good.

I remember being one of the youngest in the unit and watching the salty Marines and what they did to learn the ropes. A lot of guys would work out on the pull-ups a couple weeks before the PT (physical training) test, hoping to improve their score, but most didn't improve at all. One of my NCOs struggled with the pull-ups. I watched him do something very different than everyone else—everyday he would do pull-ups. Each time he entered the compound, he would stop at the pull-up bar and knock out as many as he could, and each time he left, he would do the same thing. Others would do it sporadically, but this guy was consistent.

One day, I watched him fill a sandbag and put it in an old ALICE pack (All-purpose Lightweight Individual Carrying Equipment standard backpack issued for the Marines of my era). He would then proceed to strap it on and do pull-ups the same way he had done before. Rain or shine, no matter what, he would hit those pull-ups. I asked him why he wore the extra weight, and he told me that pull-ups were hard to improve because you just pull the same weight each time. He told me that if he conditioned his body to pull the extra weight of the pack every time, then when it came time for the test, he could do more because his body would be pulling less weight than it had been accustomed to.

This simple lesson sticks with me. It hearkens back to the old saying, "The more you sweat in training, the less you will bleed in battle." I watched him identify a problem (not enough pull-ups), create structure around it (sandbag pull-ups), make it a routine (weighted pull-ups each time he entered or exited the compound), and have the discipline to do it every time without fail until he achieved his goal. This simple formula has helped me achieve many goals in life and has been paramount in my battle with posttraumatic stress.

In this chapter, I will break it down so you can use this same technique for any area you want to improve in your life. Structure and routine are the easy parts. Discipline will be the difference between success and failure. Okay—pack your ruck and prepare to move out.

Field Intel

> You will never change your life until you change something you do daily. The secret of your success is found in your daily routine.
> —John Maxwell

Structure, routine, and discipline form the foundation of a successful warrior and a successful person. Through this three-step process, I have found much success in battling posttraumatic stress, as well as creating a successful business, family, and a nonprofit organization.

The US military is very good at creating structure, probably better than any other organization in the world. The US military leads in creating structure. I remember in boot camp that every minute of the day is structured. From the time you wake up to the time you lay your head down, there is structure—even the manner by which you get into bed is structured. A typical day in recruit training consists of minute-by-minute structure. The typical day looks something like this:

Reveille (wake-up). The DI (drill instructor) sounds the alarm, and all recruits immediately jump out of their racks and stand at the position of attention at the end of their racks. The DI then gives the command to sound off, requiring each man to count off in a series to ensure everyone is accounted for. Directly afterward, you have a few minutes to make your rack, shave, and prepare your uniform for the day.

Physical Training. Next is physical training. Hundreds stand in formation and listen for the exercise commands the lead cadre demonstrates and repeats.

Housekeeping. Next, the unit is back to shower and clean. Each man is assigned a specific task, and like a busy bechive, everyone scurries about completing the assigned tasks with the utmost urgency.

Chow Time. The next command is to form up for chow, and everyone rushes outside to get in formation. Each man knows his place in the formation, first by squad leader, then by height. We all fall in, standing at the ready for the next command. We march in formation and in unison as if we are one unit, one body, one entity moving in rhythm with the sound of the DI's commands. We all arrive at the chow hall, each platoon led by their DI to the front doors, where we enter the building in an orderly manner in silence. With each man in line directly behind the next, we receive our morning ration of powdered eggs, unsalted grits, and a flavorless substance that resembles sausage gravy with the consistency of Jell-O and the color of sour milk.

Training. From here we commence with the training of the day, stopping only to have afternoon chow, which is administered the same as in the morning with a close formation. Each man is quick and quiet with their actions, not wanting to draw attention to himself. Next is more training until evening chow. The process never changes, no matter what hour of the day or day of the week it is.

Free Time. After evening chow, we march back to our barracks, where there is mail call and extra training of the DI's choosing. We are then given one hour of free time to prepare our uniform for the next day, read and write letters back home, or handle any personal business that may have come up.

Lights Out. The DI once again calls us to attention, and each man stands at the end of his rack and sounds off for accountability. Remember, I told you that even the way we got in bed was structured. Well, I wasn't kidding. The next command is "Prepare to mount." Each man leaves the foot of their rack and stands beside it, preparing to mount either the top or bottom rack. "Mount" is the next command in the series, telling us to climb on top of our bunk but still be at the position of attention, not moving or speaking. We lie there, and the DI has us recite something from memory, like the mission of the Marine Corps Rifle Squad or something similar. The final command, "*Aaaaadjust!*" allows the recruits to get comfortable and go to sleep.

This structure became our daily routine for twelve weeks. It is so engrained in us that when we close our eyes even now, we can hear our DI's voice in our heads. This structure and routine is very important in creating the discipline we needed in the fleet, where we have more freedom. The structure and routine served us well once we were at our units.

The expectation is the same for formations and readiness. It is this basic formula that makes us successful in the military and continues to make us successful today. We learned to create structure to solve problems and meet expectations. How are you structuring your day today? I am willing to bet you aren't.

Renowned leadership expert John C. Maxwell says, "You will

never change your life until you change something you do daily. The secret of your success is found in your daily routine."[48] So think about that now. What is your daily routine? Do you have one? Or do you just wake up and take things as they come? Do you set goals for each day, or do you just do as much as you can? Do you drive your day, or are you just a passenger in your life?

Learning to set a morning routine can drastically improve the rest of your day, relieving anxiety and depression. A quick internet search will yield thousands of results supporting the fact that a morning routine is mentally beneficial. Anxiety and depression are often linked to a feeling of a loss of control. Establishing a morning routine will help alleviate this stressor. It will also give us the fundamentals to use routine as a way to control other aspects of life, such as regaining control of our thoughts and emotions.

Once we build a routine, we can begin the process of making it routine. This usually takes about thirty days before we begin to see actual results; it also takes about thirty more days for this new structure to become conditioned in our mind. It takes the same consistency and time to rewire your neural network to accept the new routine.

The third part of the equation is discipline. This is the hardest part to maintain and the place where most failure occurs. If discipline was easy, then everyone who bought a gym membership in January would still be working out in June. But they aren't. They all want to lose weight, so they join a gym and are motivated. They decide to work out four days a week, and they even establish a routine to lose weight. By the time February rolls around, they have already missed several days because of one reason or another. By March, they are only going one day a week. By June, they stop altogether because they aren't seeing the results they want. They created structure and had a routine, but lacked the discipline to see it through.

---

[48]   https://www.awakenthegreatnesswithin.com/40-inspirational-john-c-max-well-quotes-on-success/.

Discipline and integrity are the glue that holds all other virtues together. A well-disciplined man is a successful man. You must have the discipline and self-control to adhere to your values and move toward the goals you set. Once you learn this process of SRD, you can apply it to any goal and find success. Later in this chapter, I'll show you how to create a morning routine and use that framework to overcome a barrier in your life.

Scripture Unpack

> *The mind governed by the flesh is death, but the mind governed by the Spirit is life and peace.*
> Romans 8:6 NIV

One of the biggest things I had to do was stop waiting for my symptoms to go away and accept them as a part of who I am now. I had to stop focusing on what I couldn't do and focus on what I could do—my victories. I had to start looking at my mental injury as if it was a physical one. Posttraumatic stress doesn't have to limit the things you do. You just have to learn how to do them differently.

I have a good friend and Marine brother who was paralyzed with a noncombat injury. He broke his back in a snowboarding accident and could not deploy with his team. It was devastating for him on both a personal and a professional level. Prior to the injury, he was heavily involved in extreme sports. He faced the new reality of being unable to walk, not being with his Marine brothers, and not ever participating in the sports he loved. One moment in his life changed his trajectory forever. He had a choice: give up, which he almost did, or continue to live in a new, limited way.

He chose neither. He chose to find a way to continue doing what he loved by training for the Paralympics. He came close, but did not qualify for the Paralympic team—but he took his love for sports even further. He had found his way back to the sports he loved and found healing in the process, and he didn't stop there. He began to find and train other disabled veterans to participate in the Paralympics as well. He found a way back to his brothers. He exemplifies the meaning of esprit de corps, the spirit of the Marine Corps. He knew he had limitations, but didn't focus on them. Instead, he focused on what he *could* do. He is currently a US Olympics track coach. He is an inspiration to many, me included.

We can do the same with a mental injury. Trauma wants to limit us to what we think we can't do, but we can find a work-around. We may not be able to do things the same way we used to, but we can still do *all things*, just in a different way. Yes, we can still go to rock concerts and crowded events, and we can still spend time with friends and family. We may just need to change the manner in which we do them. We can become a new person by being disciplined and motivated.

When we look to Scripture, we find numerous references to becoming a new man in Christ. Here are several:

> Therefore if anyone is in Christ, he is a new creature; the old things passed away; behold, new things have come. (2 Corinthians 5:17 NASB)

> Therefore we do not lose heart, but though our outer man is decaying, yet our inner man is being renewed day by day. (2 Corinthians 4:16 NASB)

> And I will give them one heart, and put a new spirit within them. And I will take the heart of stone out of their flesh and give them a heart of flesh. (Ezekiel 11:19 NASB)

> That which is born of the flesh is flesh, and that which is born of the Spirit is spirit. (John 3:6 NASB)

That you put off, concerning your former conduct, the old man which grows corrupt according to the deceitful lusts, and be renewed in the spirit of your mind, and that you put on the new man which was created according to God, in true righteousness and holiness. (Ephesians 4:22–24 NKJV)

Those who live according to the flesh have their minds set on what the flesh desires; but those who live in accordance with the Spirit have their minds set on what the Spirit desires. The mind governed by the flesh is death, but the mind governed by the Spirit is life and peace. The mind governed by the flesh is hostile to God; it does not submit to God's law, nor can it do so. Those who are in the realm of the flesh cannot please God. (Romans 8:5–8 NIV)

That's a lot of Scripture to illustrate one point: how you train your thought life is how you live your real life. I'd like to take time to unpack the last two.

Ephesians 4:22 says we have to *take off the old man*, our old sinful ways. Sinful ways? How about I say *your former conduct*. This refers to your old way of acting, your old way of handling problems, and your old, useless ways of dealing with posttraumatic stress and conducting yourself in the world. Let's be honest. If what you are doing is working, you probably wouldn't be reading this book. You wouldn't be searching for a better way. So you have to stop being stuck on stupid, trust there is a better way, and acknowledge the fact that self-serving behavior isn't working.

Verse 23 of Ephesians 4 says to *be renewed in the spirit of your mind*. As a Christian, we have a whole new understanding, as well as a moral and spiritual capability, that apart from God we cannot achieve. We can engage our cognitive thought process and override our deceitful, emotional subconscious min—the part that can't think apart from itself or consider other people or concepts of society and community.

Verse 24 tells us that when we surrender our life to Jesus and choose to follow Him, we become a *new creation*. As a new man according to God, righteous and holy, we can connect with God through the sacrifice of Jesus Christ by the power of the Holy Spirit working in our life. Jesus is the way to a relationship with God; therefore, we can understand more fully God's character by reading the Bible and learning about His attributes.

In his letter to the Romans, Paul echoes these same truths. In Romans 8:5 (ESV), he says, "For those who live according to the flesh set their minds on the things of the flesh, but those who live according to the Spirit set their minds on the things of the Spirit." He tells us that how we act is directly correlated to how we think, and when we think in the flesh (worldly ideas and desires), we will live in the same manner. However, if we transition our mind to the things of God—to kingdom-minded, spiritual desires—we in turn will live as such.

Verse 6 says the mind focused on the flesh, or worldly desires, will bring death—not necessarily physical death, but spiritual death—and to be kingdom-minded will bring peace and life. He accentuates the point in verse 7, where he says that the worldly desires of our carnal mind focused on serving self are at odds with the Holy Spirit and are hostile toward God. Verse 8 tells us that a mind continually focused on worldly things cannot please God.

These two letters by Paul are central to the next part of our exercises. When your life fully realizes and manifests this concept, you will be well on your way to overcoming the traumas you've experienced.

We talked about the placebo effect earlier in the book, and here we'll unpack it a bit more. It's a fascinating medical anomaly in which a patient thinks they're receiving a specific medication, but they're actually not receiving any medication whatsoever. Nevertheless, the patient experiences the medication's physical effects. WebMD explains it like this:

> Sometimes a person can have a response to a placebo. The response can be positive or negative. For instance, the person's symptoms may improve. Or the person may have what appears to be side effects from the treatment. These responses are known as the 'placebo effect.'
>
> There are some conditions in which a placebo can produce results even when people know they are taking a placebo. Studies show that placebos can have an effect on conditions such as depression, pain, sleep disorders, irritable bowel syndrome, [and] menopause. In one study involving asthma, people using a placebo inhaler did no better on breathing tests than [when they were] sitting and doing nothing. But when researchers asked for people's perception of how they felt, the placebo inhaler was reported as being as effective as medicine in providing relief.
>
> How Does the Placebo Effect Work?
>
> Research on the placebo effect has focused on the relationship of mind and body. One of the most common theories is that the placebo effect is due to a person's expectations. If a person expects a pill to do something, then it's possible that the body's own chemistry can cause effects similar to what a medication might have caused.
>
> For instance, in one study, people were given a placebo and told it was a stimulant. After taking the pill, their pulse rate sped up, their blood pressure increased, and their reaction speed improved. When people were

given the same pill and told it was to help them get to sleep, they experienced the opposite effects.

Experts also say that there is a relationship between how strongly a person expects to have results and whether or not results occur. The stronger the feeling, the more likely it is that a person will experience positive effects. There may be a profound effect due to the interaction between a patient and healthcare provider.[49]

Another study published in 2014 in *Science Translational Medicine* explored this by testing how people reacted to migraine pain medication. One group took a migraine drug labeled with the drug's name, another took a placebo labeled "placebo," and a third group took nothing. The researchers discovered that the placebo was 50 percent as effective as the real drug in reducing pain after a migraine attack. The same appears to be true for negative effects. If people expect to have side effects such as headaches, nausea, or drowsiness, there is a greater chance of those reactions happening.[50]

The fact that the placebo effect is tied to expectations doesn't make it imaginary or fake. Some studies show that there are actual physical changes that occur with the placebo effect. For instance, some studies have documented an increase in the body's production of endorphins, one of the body's natural pain relievers.

One problem with the placebo effect is that it can be difficult to distinguish from the actual effects of a real drug during a study. Finding ways to distinguish between the placebo effect and the effect of treatment may help improve the treatment and lower the cost of

[49] DerSarkissian, "The Placebo Effect: What Is It?"
[50] Slavenka Kam-Hansen, Moshe Jakubowski, John M. Kelley, Irving Kirsch, David C. Hoaglin, Ted J. Kaptchuk, and Rami Burstein, "Altered Placebo and Drug Labeling Changes the Outcome of Episodic Migraine Attacks." *Science Translational Medicine*, U.S. National Library of Medicine, January 8, 2014, www.ncbi.nlm.nih.gov/pubmed/24401940.

drug testing. And more study may also lead to ways to use the power of the placebo effect in treating disease.[51]

What does this tell us? Your own thoughts create a chemical reaction in your body that mimics the medication results based upon your own expectations. That's amazing! So what does the Bible say about this? "And be not conformed to this world: but be ye transformed by the renewing of your mind" (Romans 12:2 KJV).

Set your mind on the things of God and not of this world. Your weaknesses God can use for His glory, but you must be willing to share them. Knowledge is wasted until it is shared.

In the next section, we will uncover a three-step process that will help you focus your mind using everything you have learned so far.

Tactical Application

I am no longer a slave to addiction or a slave to my emotions, no longer a slave to my subconscious mind.

—Sgt Q

Here is where we apply training to initiate your brain's ability to move from operating in an emotional state to a cognitive one. This is not a new idea, but one that's been used for decades and one that the Bible mentions. Ask yourself, *How far down the rabbit hole do I want to go?* From here, things get very obscure, and you will no doubt have many more questions than I have answers.

Let's look at another example of creating the right mindset through an experiment that was conducted in 1980 by the International Peace Project. During the Israeli-Lebanese war, they trained people in the region to feel peace in their bodies rather than just think and pray for peace to occur. At specific times and on specific days, these people did as they were trained, and the data was recorded. There were quantifiable results that showed vio-

[51] DerSarkissian, "The Placebo Effect: What Is It?"

lence decreased during the window of the experiment. The results were published in the *Journal of Conflict Resolution* in 1988: "Our thoughts and intentions have a greater effect not only on our bodies, but on others, and by proxy, the world as a whole."[52]

This led me to further investigate how they were praying to have this effect. I found answers of how to pray in a small book called the *Secrets of the Lost Mode of Prayer*, by Gregg Braden. He says that when we pray, we need to believe our words.

> Any uncertainty I may have had regarding how this principle works disappeared on a day in the early '90s. It had been a time of extreme drought in the high deserts of northern New Mexico, when my native friend David (not his real name) invited me to an ancient stone circle to "pray rain."[53]

The story goes that the Native American knelt down on the ground and bowed his head. After a few minutes he stood up and said he was finished. Somewhat perplexed by the lack of exuberance in the prayer, Braden asked about the event. His friend then explained that he did not pray for rain, but rather "prayed rain." He envisioned the rain falling and the sights and sounds of the rain. He imagined the smell and the end results from a fresh rain.

After reading this story of a Native American mode of prayer, I wanted to see if there was any scriptural basis for this type of event. I found it in the book of James as the writer referenced the story of Elijah in 1 Kings:

> Therefore confess your sins to each other and pray for
> each other so that you may be healed. The prayer of a

---

[52] Shapiro, Robert Y. and Benjamin I. Page, "Foreign Policy and the Rational Public," *The Journal of Conflict Resolution*, vol. 32, no. 2, 1988, pp. 211–247. JSTOR, www.jstor.org/stable/174045.
[53] Gregg Braden, *Secrets of the Lost Mode of Prayer: The Hidden Power of Beauty, Blessing, Wisdom, and Hurt*, Hay House, Inc., 2006.

righteous person is powerful and effective. Elijah was a human being, even as we are. He prayed earnestly that it would not rain, and it did not rain on the land for three and a half years. Again he prayed, and the heavens gave rain, and the earth produced its crops. (James 5:16–18 NIV)

So Elijah prayed for there to be a drought, and then three and a half years later he prays for rain, and it rains! This is intriguing, so I studied further. How was he able to do this? Let's look at the book of 1 Kings. "Now Elijah the Tishbite, of Tishbe in Gilead, said to Ahab, 'As the LORD, the God of Israel, lives, before whom I stand, there shall be neither dew nor rain these years, except by my word'" (1 Kings 17:1 ESV). Elijah declares that no rain shall fall on the land unless by his word. This is a bold statement indeed. He then departs the land, only to return three and a half years later, after there has been a severe drought in the land. When he returns, he is challenged by the false prophets of Baal and calls fire down from heaven!

This dude called for fire from heaven upon the enemy (1 Kings 18:37–39). I mention this because it would seem that Elijah was the first ANGLICO Marine, calling fire on an enemy position. I don't know if anyone else saw this little nugget, but here it is. From here he goes to a mountain to "pray rain."

And Elijah said to Ahab, "Go up, eat and drink, for there is a sound of the rushing of rain." So Ahab went up to eat and to drink. And Elijah went up to the top of Mount Carmel. And he bowed himself down on the earth and put his face between his knees. And he said to his servant, "Go up now, look toward the sea." And he went up and looked and said, "There is nothing." And he said, "Go again," seven times. And at the seventh time he said, "Behold, a little cloud like a man's hand is rising from the sea." And he said, "Go up, say to Ahab, 'Prepare your chariot and go down, lest the rain stop you.'" And in a little while the heavens grew black with clouds and wind, and there was a great rain. And Ahab rode and went to Jezreel. And the hand of the LORD was on Elijah, and he gathered up his garment and ran before Ahab to the entrance of Jezreel. (1 Kings 18:41–46 ESV)

The story of the Native American prayer and the recording of Elijah's prayer in Holy Scripture are very similar. I wonder if Elijah had similar thoughts as he prayed seven times. Did he remember what the rain smells and feels like? Did he focus on these sensations and this became his prayer?

I took this new concept, along with what I learned in my research about the placebo effect and similar studies, and measured it against what I had learned from the Bible. If you have any doubt how this lines up with Scripture, I would invite you to go back to the multiple Scriptures I have laid out in this section and study them, as I have, and come to your own conclusion.

Further investigation reveals research showing that gratitude and appreciation release powerful hormones in our bodies and strengthen our immune systems.

To overcome posttraumatic stress, I have used the following three-step process:

1. Structure: Renew the mind. I take whatever problem I am facing, and I restructure it into something useful. I focus less on the problem and more on the solution. The book of James speaks a lot on this subject. "Count it all joy . . . when you meet trials of various kinds" (James 1:2 ESV). I spoke at length about this earlier in the book. Now you will see how to use this to create structure. We can't focus on what we can't do, but what we can. We make that our focus.

2. Routine: Become a new man. I became a new man when I surrendered and made a conscious choice to follow Jesus Christ. "Therefore if any man be in Christ, he is a new creature: old things are passed away; behold, all things are become new" (2 Corinthians 5:17 KJV). Putting this into practice involves conscious decision-making to change my thinking and my behavior.

Anything I want to accomplish in this world I must first accomplish in my mind and will. When I could see this in my mind, my imagination, I could then bring it into reality. This is a process all great inventors used. They would picture their invention in their mind and then bring it to reality by putting it on paper. Next they would build three-dimensional models, and finally the prototype.

The process of becoming a new man unfortunately does not happen overnight. It is a long process of consistently making decisions that follow Jesus and align with the goal. There is no compromise on the routine. This must be upheld to see any benefits from our work. On average, it takes sixty-six days for something to become a routine, but it can vary anywhere from 18 to 254 days, so don't give up.

3. Discipline: Faith in action. Again, the book of James tells us about how our actions develop our faith. Faith without works is dead (James 2:14–26). This is where many fail, but don't lose heart. Pick yourself up and try again. Don't give up, and your life will be filled with constant improvement. A good friend and mentor of mine, George Wade, says, "Take a knee, drink some water, and suck it up." That's good advice. Take a knee, a break, or a rest period to reevaluate and muster the energy to try again. Drink some water, and become refreshed and filled with one of the core elements we need to survive—you could also say, "Be filled with the living water" (there is a sermon in here, but I'll save that for later). Then you suck it up; you try again.

I'll give you an example from my life: when I decided to stop drinking. There are a lot of great programs out there to help with alcohol and other addictions, and they have great success helping people kick their addictions. I did not use one of those programs. I simply used structure, routine, and discipline to overcome my alcohol addiction. I am not suggesting this approach will work for everyone, but it did have amazing results for me. I created structure around my drinking. First, I made the conscious decision to stop drinking, and I told others about it. Second, I stopped hanging out with people who drank. I stopped playing pool in bars where everyone was drinking. Third, I knew I needed to replace the negative behavior with a positive one, so every time I wanted to drink, I drank orange juice instead. Why orange juice? I don't know; it just seemed like a good substitution for the whiskey sours I was accustomed to drinking. I must have drunk a gallon of orange juice every week, so over fifty gallons per year. That's a lot of orange juice! Here's what it looked like when I used this process.

Goal: Stop abusing alcohol.

Structure: Stop drinking. Tell others I have stopped drinking so they can hold me accountable. I had to set small goals for myself. One week became two weeks, then a month, three months, six months, a year. A lot of other programs use this goal-setting method, and coins are handed out for reaching milestones. I just kept a record of it and used the record to help me keep from breaking my streak. The longer I went, the more I didn't want to start over from day one. There were a few times I did fail and had to start over, but I never quit trying. Making the structure was the easy part. The process can take several months, but with enough desire you can get there. If you know you should do it but lack the desire, pray to the Lord for the power to stop the addiction. Pray daily, pray all the time, and lean on Him. He's the one who can help you transform your life.

Routine: Stop going to places where people drink. Stop hanging out with people who drink. I had to do the same thing the same way every day. I avoided liquor stores on my way home from work. Ignore the invites from friends to go and party.

Discipline: Replacing the negative behavior (drinking alcohol) with a positive one (drinking orange juice) helps you to stick with it. Every time I felt like having a drink, I would have a glass or two of orange juice. Anytime I had a craving, I would drink orange juice. I would buy it everywhere—the gas station, grocery store, and from a restaurant. It didn't matter where I was; I could avoid alcohol. I did it every time I had a craving until it just became automatic. This is where endurance, conviction, and intestinal fortitude came into play.

Remember the gym rat example in chapter 2? We see that it's easy to create structure and routine, but what most people lack is discipline—the ability to endure hardship for long periods of time to achieve a goal. Denying and delaying gratification for yourself are not things that come naturally. We are very much a me-first, right-now society, so when we choose to change that behavior, it becomes a hardship. It is difficult and uncomfortable. You won't like it. It'll hurt, but in pain there is growth.

For many years, I avoided people and places that had anything to do with alcohol because I was weak and didn't want to stumble back into the lifestyle I once had. Now I'm much stronger and am able to be in the presence of those who are drinking without experiencing cravings. I've conditioned my flesh to the point of submission to my conscious mind. In my old life, I couldn't just enjoy a drink at dinner. I would have to drink in excess every time. Once that poison got into my system, the rails came off, and I reverted to those thoughts, feelings, emotions, and trauma.

I am so thankful to God that I do not live like that anymore. I am no longer a slave to addiction or a slave to my emotions, and I am no longer a slave to my subconscious mind. It has been ten years since I've experienced drunkenness, and I'm overjoyed at my progress. But it took years for me to get to this point. I suggest you do the same with something you feel is holding you back. Use these steps:

1. Identify the problem.
2. Create a plan and find someone who can hold you accountable for progress (Structure).
3. Identify the triggers and eliminate them. Once you eliminate them, do not look back and regret your choice, so you don't become bound to those triggers (Routine).
4. Create attainable goals that can be progressively reached. One day, one week, one month, three months, six months, one year. Creating structured benchmarks and goals, along with having an accountability partner, will help ensure your success and longevity (Discipline).

Debrief

A well-disciplined soldier will be victorious. In the military, we are disciplined and intentional with our actions. It is discipline that allows us to move forward in battle and not run into the face of danger. For most of us, on the battlefield we are good, and some are great. It isn't until we leave the battlefield that we begin to struggle. We try to leave that warrior on the battlefield. We try to forget all the things we've learned and discard our warrior mindset. We want to return home and fit in. So now let me ask, How has that been working out for you?

The old warrior is left behind, and you are now a new man, but that doesn't mean all the lessons you learned need to be forgotten. There are valuable tactics you can use from past training: discipline in your actions, obedience to God, strength in numbers, and courage under fire. All these things you learned can help you be successful in this new war of your mind.

The Spartans and the Vikings both possessed this discipline, and it served them well on the battlefield. The Spartans formed a phalanx when faced with the enemy. This wedge formation was where the warrior's shield protected the man to the left and the sword protected the man on the right. Be disciplined and use the prayer you develop to create a wedge between yourself and the enemy. Be disciplined and study the Word of God to add weapons to your arsenal. Be relentless and disciplined in your thoughts. Thoughts become your actions, your actions become your conduct, and your conduct becomes your character.

If you want to be better at anything, you must put in the work. Remember the operator's mentality—smooth is fast, and fast is smooth. Do the small things well, and the big things will come easier. You think, therefore you become, so be disciplined in your thoughts and conform you mind to the thoughts of God.

You cannot forget the lessons you learned on the battlefield; however, you must accept who you are now. Don't mourn for the person you used to be. My healing didn't begin until I chose to accept the fact that I'm now a different person—I'm no longer just a Marine, a warfighter. That person I was died in Iraq, and I had to let him go. That person is never coming back. I wasted a lot of my time and energy spinning my wheels trying to raise the dead. I literally mourned for myself, for who I was that died on the battlefield, yet I'm still here. I had to let go of the old person and find a new identity. Who was I now?

I found my identity in Christ, and with that identity came a new mission. Like the phoenix, I had to rise from the ashes of my old life and become a new creation.

CHAPTER 11

HEALING THRU SERVICE

*When we can get outside our own personal pain and
struggle to help others, it fundamentally changes the chemical structure of our brain.*
—Sgt Q

Personal Recon

THE FINAL LESSON. EVERYTHING WE'VE BEEN learning leads us to this
point. All the study of the brain and how it operates, the effects of
trauma on our mind, body, and spirit, and the exercises to overcome the symptoms of posttraumatic stress: this chapter will show
you how to live these things out in a new way. The entire book
could have been simply about this one concept, this one chapter,

but if I didn't give you the background, then this lesson could easily be dismissed.

Now that you understand how our brain operates and you've been practicing the methods to take back control of your mind, this next section will have more value in your life. The real key to long-lasting healing is helping others. We call it Healing thru Service.

Seems too simple, right?

Healing thru Service is the QMissions motto, but for me and others like me, it's not just a slogan; it's become a way of life. When we can get outside our personal pain and struggle to help others, it fundamentally changes the chemical structure of our brain. I first noticed this when I went to Mexico and built a house for a homeless family. It was then I realized that something inside me was changing, but I didn't quite know what it was. I came back feeling different. I didn't know what was happening, but I knew I wanted to keep going.

I attended several of these trips over the next few years. Each year, I'd spend thousands of dollars and multiple weeks participating in three to four of these building missions. It wasn't easy. I had to sacrifice a lot to go on these missions—my free time, my money, and my comfort. On these trips, I'd experience a lot of anxiety and panic attacks, sleepless nights, and horrible digestive issues. I'd travel overseas for a couple weeks serving an impoverished community. It was rewarding, but it was also healing me—even though I couldn't truly recognize it at the time.

My service didn't end when I crossed back over the border. While at home, I also served at my local church. Every Sunday I'd work with a small team that would arrive before anyone else and help set up for the day's events. We'd also help rearrange the chairs between the three services. It was backbreaking work to move hundreds of chairs in and out of the auditorium every ninety minutes, but someone had to do it. I moved chairs for two years until a new building was built and moving the chairs was no longer necessary. I also served evenings in youth ministry with two others. We'd cook a meal for the high schoolers attending the evening service.

I continued this service for many years until God called me to another church where I continue to serve in their children's ministry. I also joined some of my friends to make lunches and snacks, then deliver them on the street, loving on some of the most vulnerable in our society—the homeless. From there we hooked up with a local homeless encampment and helped them build infrastructure to get out of the rain. These encampments were well run and policed by the people living in them. The majority of those living in the camp had regular jobs, but had fallen on hard times. Their spirits were undeterred by their circumstances. Soon after working in the camps, my family and I joined the Salvation Army in their mission to provide a hot meal for anyone who needed it. It was a successful program that brought a sense of community to the neighborhood.

This constant service to others helped me overcome the effects of war, and I didn't even fully realize it until 2015, when God called me to start QMissions and direct my efforts to help other veterans find the same healing I experienced.

I wish I could say that I was excited and jumped at the opportunity, but that's not reality. The truth is I didn't want to do it. It seemed like a lot of work, and I had already been through so much. I just wanted to take it easy, so I did. For months, I refused to help other veterans. I had plenty of excuses. I wasn't some war hero. I didn't have the time or money. I wanted an easy life free from more responsibility. I still struggled with my posttraumatic stress, so how could I help anyone else? I used all these things to refuse the calling God had for me.

That all changed one morning when I received a message that one of my Marines had "gone off the grid." This is a common term we use to signify someone is missing. Usually when we find them, they've committed suicide. It was a very solemn experience to read on the internet about all the military members who have gone off the grid and the accounts of their brothers looking for them. I prayed to God that he would be found alive. I didn't want his death to be the catalyst for me to start this mission, so I consciously decided that whether he lived or died, I would help other veterans. Three days later, my brother was found alive. He'd checked himself into the VA hospital. It was only six months after the commitment that I led my first team of veterans on Operation Restore Hope in Mexico.

Since then, we've deployed several times to Mexico, Kenya, and Cambodia, with missions planned for Brazil, the Philippines, and Suriname in the coming year. God didn't just want me to take veterans overseas, but He also wanted me to teach them all the lessons I had learned along the way. This has been a much more daunting task, and this book is part of the evolution of my healing.

These things you are reading are part of the curriculum that is taught when I take veterans to Mexico. We build a home for a homeless family in two days with the help and support of the YWAM ministry Homes of Hope, and we use this home build as a tool to overcome posttraumatic stress with Healing thru Service. The results have been remarkable. We've been recognized by the Department of Veterans Affairs and have received multiple awards for the success veterans have found through the program. In 2017, Seattle's KIRO 7 News honored our efforts by naming me Seattle's Hometown Hero. Sure, I knew the process God put me through worked for me, but I couldn't have imagined the impact it would have on others. Every veteran God sends my way is put through the same process I went through—starting with building a home in Mexico.

Field Intel

As I mentioned, QMissions has received multiple awards for the program Operation Restore Hope. It's a beautiful way to begin the healing process, and one that has recently been backed up by science. *Psychology Today* reported on a 2016 study:

> "The Neurobiology of Giving Versus Receiving Support: The Role of Stress-Related and Social Reward-Related Neural Activity" was published in *Psychosomatic Medicine: Journal of Biobehavioral Medicine*. The lead researchers of this study were Tristen Inagaki, Ph.D., from the University of Pittsburgh and Naomi Eisenberger, Ph.D., of University of California, Los Angeles (UCLA).[54]

During this study, "participants were asked about various scenarios in which they either gave or received social support. For example, having 'someone to lean on' or 'looking for ways to cheer people up' when they were feeling down."[55] The researchers looked at brain scan images taken during the interviews. Something amazing appeared in the results.

"As would be expected, both giving and receiving social support correlated to lower reported negative psychosocial outcomes."[56] However, the MRI neuroimaging tests that explored the neural mechanisms showed something else. The researchers were able to look at the specific areas of the brain affected during the interview. They concluded that giving social support ultimately had greater brain benefits than receiving it.[57]

Giving social support also had profound effects on the reduction of stress-related activity in the dorsal anterior cingulate cortex, the right anterior insula, and the right amygdala. Yes! The amygdala.

[54] Christopher Bergland, "Three Specific Ways that Helping Others Benefits Your Brain," *Psychology Today*, February 21, 2016, https://www.psychologytoday.com/us/blog/the-athletes-way/201602/3-specific-ways-helping-others-benefits-your-brain.
[55] Bergland, "Three Specific Ways that Helping Others Benefits Your Brain."
[56] Bergland, "Three Specific Ways that Helping Others Benefits Your Brain."
[57] Bergland, "Three Specific Ways that Helping Others Benefits Your Brain."

Remember that primitive little area of the brain that likes to hijack us by causing a panic attack? There was also greater reward-related activity in the left and right ventral striatum, as well as greater care-giving-related activity in the septal area.

In all of these brain areas, fMRI scans showed specific activation when a participant was giving support, but not when receiving support. For example, the researchers found that while performing a stressful mental math task, participants who gave the most support had reduced activation in brain areas related to stress responses. However, the person receiving support on a math problem didn't display activation in stress-related brain regions.

Also, giving social support was associated with increased activity in a brain area that functions as part of the reward system during an "affiliative" task. These changes within the brain help to explain why altruism and giving support has multiple health benefits.

On a neurobiological level, this research pinpoints specific ways that when you help others, you're also helping yourself. The rewards of giving and receiving social support creates the ultimate win-win situation. When someone in need receives help, he or she benefits directly from the social support; simultaneously, the giver benefits in specific brain regions associated with stress, reward, and caregiving. . . .

These results add to emerging literature suggesting that support giving is an overlooked contributor to how social support can benefit health. The findings question the conventional idea that the health benefits of social support mainly reflect received support.

At the level of the brain, only support giving was

associated with beneficial outcomes by reducing activity in stress- and threat-related regions during stressful experiences. Giving support, on the other hand, allows an individual to control when and how support is given . . . [and] may result in more effective stress reduction. . . .

Conclusion: Generosity and Gratitude Create an Upward Spiral of Well-Being

The findings of this new study suggest that the overall health benefits of giving social support have specific roots in various brain regions. The findings also suggest that giving support is part of a feedback loop that makes giving social support rewarding to the giver. This is a generous biological design that is probably key to our survival and well-being as a species.[58]

Well, would you look at that! This Healing thru Service thing is actually quantifiable! I have to admit it's pretty cool to see science back up what God has been teaching us all along.

Another very interesting study was conducted by the Army over a period of forty years. This study set out to determine the greatest factor for success on the battlefield. Their conclusion was this: the squad mentality.

The creation of effective fireteams [squads] is seen as essential for creating an effective professional military as they serve as a primary group. Psychological studies by the United States Army have indicated that the willingness to fight is more heavily influenced by the desire to avoid failing to provide support to other members of the fireteam than by abstract concepts. Historically, nations with effective fireteam organization have had significantly better performance from their infantry

---

[58] Bergland, "Three Specific Ways that Helping Others Benefits Your Brain."

units in combat than those limited to operations by larger units.[59]

So basically, the squad performs because the individual members are motivated to not let down the squad. *Huh?* Seems that the Army has figured out what God has been telling us for generations. Amazing!

The fact that we fight in small squads becomes the driving force behind our victories. Each man in the squad values the squad over himself, and therefore will fight harder and longer to not let the rest of the squad down. They may want to quit on themselves, but they will not quit on the squad. This is an important lesson to remember and to take into our battle with posttraumatic stress and the daily battles we all face in this life. Working together toward a common goal is a surefire way to be successful. It has been proven time and time again throughout history. Take this lesson into your daily life and begin to build a squad of people you trust, and work together toward a common goal.

Like the improvement of your street, your community, or the work of your hand, the survival of a squad member requires support. It is very important to create a support network for yourself and others. It can be as simple as a couple guys you can depend on to help you get through the rough patches in life. Whatever the size, an accountability group that makes sure all the members are moving forward—not getting lost in the system or in their posttraumatic stress symptoms—will improve the likelihood of success. I have my own group of guys that hold me accountable to the standards I set for myself. They are also there to look out for me when they see me getting off track. I feel I can go to them when I'm struggling in my head and suffering in silence too. We didn't fight the war alone, so we shouldn't think we can fight the trauma alone either.

---

[59] https://military.wikia.org/wiki/Fireteam.

Scripture Unpack

In Ecclesiastes, the author shows us the value of a friend as a great way to succeed in life:

> Two are better than one, because they have a good reward for their labor. For if they fall, one will lift up his companion. But woe to him who is alone when he falls, for he has no one to help him up. Again, if two lie down together, they will keep warm; But how can one be warm alone? Though one may be overpowered by another, two can withstand him. And a threefold cord is not quickly broken. (Ecclesiastes 4:9–12 NKJV)

This process of Healing thru Service can work for anyone, but it works best when we're working together in a group or a squad. God tells us to live in fellowship with one another. These verses articulate it very well. They tell us woe to the man who is alone. You see, the enemy wants us to be alone so we can be easily overtaken. Posttraumatic stress causes us to isolate from others, so we must fight to stay connected to others. When we're helping someone else, we're not alone—it's a great consequence of helping and serving others.

Is it starting to come together now? I'll give you an example from history that will add a couple more colors to the picture.

For relatability, let's look again at the Vikings and their Shield Wall. The virtues the Viking culture taught helped make them a formidable enemy on the battlefield. These principles were instrumental in their battle tactics. Two standard formations were the Shield Wall and the Boar's Snout. The Shield Wall consisted of men lined up shoulder to shoulder with their shields interlocked to protect the men on the left and the right. Each man knew that if he failed, he would put the entire team in jeopardy. They worked as a team—one unit, one goal. If a man was wounded, the men to the left and right would hold him up. They'd do this until the man could be replaced in the Shield Wall, and then they'd move him to the rear for medical treatment.

The Huscarls would move from the rear of the formation and help lift the wounded man. The Huscarls were the king's elite men and the biggest and strongest men on the battlefield, akin to today's Special Forces. Regardless, the formation could continue forward. They knew their greatest strength was fighting together as one unit, and if anyone got separated, it would mean certain death for all of them.[60]

None of us fought a war by ourselves, so why would we fight posttraumatic stress alone? Lean on your brothers and sisters when you're struggling. Lift one another up in prayer when you see them stumbling. Be disciplined and work as a team.

Tactical Application

God will move you to an area to serve where your testi-
mony will have the greatest impact. This will cause you to
expand your reach in new, more challenging ways.
—Sgt Q

Go to work. Start serving. It doesn't matter where, or for whom; just start. A quick Google search will yield thousands of volunteer opportunities in your local community. You don't have to find the "right one" on the first attempt; any one of them will do. Just jump in and serve. Serve without any expectation of reward or accolades. This will minimize any resentment or bitterness that could well up inside you. You must have a good frame of heart when serving, which is another reason I have spent so much time covering how the brain operates. Know full well that once you are serving in an organization, there will be things you can see to make improvements, or people who are not quite the leaders you would hope

---

[60] "The Viking Age," *The Quarterly Review* (London: William Clouse and Sons), 1890.

them to be. It's okay. You're there to serve, not accomplish another agenda. You'll always have people who are struggling as leaders, so instead of chipping away at their authority, seek instead to support their ideas and help them succeed, even if you don't think they will. Grasping the servant's heart is a difficult task, but once mastered, it will open many amazing doors for you.

If you attend church, then become involved with the events and programs they're championing. This servant's heart comes in handy too. If you don't know what ministry is right for you, start in the children's ministry. They always need help, and if you're a new Christian, you'll be able to learn all the Bible stories in an easy to understand format. You'll learn the jargon and songs. It's a great way to learn, along with being a rewarding experience.

As you begin to grow in your confidence and ability and assume your new identity, God will move you to an area to serve where your testimony will have the greatest impact. This will cause you to expand your reach in new, more challenging ways. Often, our testimony is born out of adversity, and the byproduct is pain. So you'll have to walk through some of that to develop into the man or woman God created you to be.

When people say to me, "I don't know what ministry God has for me," I tell them, "Look for your pain, and there your ministry will be also." I suffer with PTSD, so God has called me to help others in this area. If you have experienced trauma and are recovering, then who better to lead others to that same healing. This is exactly what I have been doing in this book and when I lead men onto the mission field. I know some of you aren't ready for that, but don't worry, you'll get there.

The best way to jump in and kick-start your healing process is to come on mission with QMissions. Sign up—it's easy. Go to our webpage, https://www.qmissions.org/, and click the link. It will give you perspective about Operation Restore Hope, as well as a gear list, code of conduct, and additional resources to prepare you for the journey. No one comes back from this mission the same.

It's a great way to jump-start your healing, like so many others have done before you. You'll have to sacrifice your time, money, and some of your comfort, but what you reap will be well worth it.

Building a team to serve with us is much easier than going it alone. Here are a few ways you can start:

1. Use this book as a resource to start your own squad.
2. Teach the fundamentals to others now that you've gone through the book. Start with some buddies who have similar interests. This will help overcome some of the fear associated with trying something new, and you'll develop new friendships along the way.
3. Lead a small group of others through this process, with the book as a resource. You don't have to be proficient at the tactics in this book; you just have to try. You can even sign your group up to go on an Operation Restore Hope mission to Mexico. It's a big step, but one that will change your life forever.

Debrief

Now that God has given me a full-time ministry, it's exhausting, complex, and hard because it's all day, all the time. There's no end of shift, no clock-out time, but the military had prepared me for this, and now I must prepare you as well. Know that as soon as you begin this journey, you will face challenges. I knew that with this ministry would come opposition. I knew the enemy would come for me.

In the Marines we have a term—*skyline*, or *don't skyline yourself.*

What does that mean? When on patrol, you never want to crest over the top of a mountain or hill. When you do this, your silhouette is easily noticed against the stark contrast of the sky behind you. We're taught to patrol below the skyline so the enemy can't see us behind the mountain. Even if you're in front of the enemy, it will be difficult for them to pick you up among the terrain and foliage as long as you stay on the front face of the mountain. The moment you cross above the skyline, you become an easy target.

The same can be said about our Christian walk. If we choose to live a quiet, unassuming life, we walk below the skyline, and for some people, this is their chosen path. However, we can choose to be bold in our faith and strong in our convictions, choosing to walk atop the mountain, exposing ourselves for the enemy to see. When we choose to do big and bold things for God, we skyline ourselves and should expect constant and relentless attacks from the enemy. So the way I see it, you have two choices: Walk below the skyline and avoid confrontation, or skyline yourself and prepare for battle. *I choose to battle!*

If you're among those who decide to put on the full armor of God (Ephesians 6) and skyline themselves on this new battlefield, here are some words of encouragement. If God is sending you somewhere, it's because there's a battle to be waged. Some of you have forgotten. I had forgotten that! When we go on patrol, we're looking for a fight. When we step out our door, we're looking for a fight—but we do not war against flesh and blood (verse 12).

- God says, "Go pray for that person," but you're afraid of embarrassment.
- A friend criticized you, and now you want to retaliate because you're wounded.
- That secret sin overpowers you, and now you carry the shame of sin like it's a ball and chain.

These are just three examples of how the devil is attacking you. Will you fold up like a lawn chair or fight back? Don't let fear cripple you. Marines, when you're told to liberate a village, do you cower from the confrontation with the enemy? No, you know the enemy is there, and that's why they're sending you.

It's the same when God calls you to go pray for someone. He

calls upon you because there's an enemy. If God is calling you to serve in an area, they must need reinforcements. We are battle-tested warriors, and we hold the line. I don't know about you, but I have never backed down from a fight in my life, and I'm not starting now. I don't care about what I did up to this point in my life. I care about what I do for the rest of my life.

Sgt Q, out.

Scripture Meditation

But whose delight is in the law of the Lord, and who meditates on his law day and night. (Psalm 1:2 NIV)

Tremble and do not sin; when you are on your beds, search your hearts and be silent. (Psalm 4:4 NIV)

May these words of my mouth and this meditation of my heart be pleasing in your sight, Lord, my Rock and my Redeemer. (Psalm 19:14 NIV)

My mouth will speak words of wisdom; the meditation of my heart will give you understanding. (Psalm 49:3 NIV)

On my bed I remember you; I think of you through the watches of the night. (Psalm 63:6 NIV)

May my meditation be pleasing to him, as I rejoice in the Lord. (Psalm 104:34 NIV)

I meditate on your precepts and consider your ways. (Psalm 119:15 NIV)

May the arrogant be put to shame for wronging me without cause; but I will meditate on your precepts. (Psalm 119:78 NIV)

My eyes stay open through the watches of the night, that I may meditate on your promises. (Psalm 119:148 NIV)

I remember the days of long ago; I meditate on all your works and consider what your hands have done. (Psalm 143:5 NIV)

Sgt Q Journal Entries

AWAKE. SICK. STRESSED. MY BRAIN WON'T stop. The stress monster is messing me up. I am my mind. Foggy. Confused. Tired. This event I am trying to put together. The stress has finally come. I knew it would come. I've been waiting for it. And now it is here. Like sitting on an OP and watching the sun disappear behind the mountains. You have heard the chatter on the coms that the enemy is amassing in the valley below and you know they will make their move under the cover of darkness, so as the last point of light escapes from the darkness of the valley, so now does the light of the lantern escape from my soul.

You wait now in nervous anticipation. We all deal with it. We all struggle with it.

This feeling of impending doom. Stress hits us and our body responds like it's a life or death situation. Our chest gets tight and our blood runs cold. But our body feels hot. So hot. Why is it so dam hot right now! I peel back the covers and gasp for air. I have sweated through the sheets and pillow. I look at my wife still bundled up from the night air chill. Three times the blankets and cozy. But me, I'm a hot mess right now. I feel sick to my stomach and my head is pounding.

IT'S 0149 IN THE MORNING AND the enemy is at the gates. Before when this would happen, I would take three or four shots of whiskey and chug a glass of water with four Advil. And it's another reason I used to drink till I passed out. To avoid these 1 and 2 a.m. wake-up calls. I have put all that behind me. Breathe, man, just breathe. Use your breathing. I give myself commands as if I am one of the Marines on patrol.

0210. I HAVE LOWERED MY HEART rate and turned off the cortisol pumping through my veins. I use a hippie breathing technique to visualize and breathe my way through [I will blog this technique another time]. Oh man, if those CA hippies I grew up with were reading this, I would never hear the end of it. I am also writing. I find that it is the hardest thing for me to do. Mostly because my brain has a hard time forming coherent thoughts. Everything is foggy and feels jumbled. Part of the PTS is that my mind won't shut off. It will keep processing and planning an attempt to prepare for any situation that may pop up. I hate surprises and I mean hate them. If you want to throw me a surprise party, don't! Even when my wife surprises me with a nice gift, I hate it. I love the gift but hate the surprise.

0240 AND I AM READY TO try to get some rack time. Don't feel sorry for me. Just seek to understand me and that, at times, everyday normal things can be overwhelming to me. Pray for me. Really just pray for me. Please. Lift me up in prayer. Intercede on my behalf before the Father. And just keep your word. If you commit to something, then follow through. This affects me more than anything else you can do. If we have a relationship, just know I will judge you most harshly on this one factor—keeping your word. In combat I depend on my men to cover their end. Cover their fields of fire and prevent the enemy from getting in the wire. If I call for evac or resupply, that chopper better be there. In this day and age, people keeping their word is a trivial matter at best, but for me and other veterans like me, it is paramount. When you don't, it is like falling asleep while on post. I can rationalize that you did not put my life in danger, but *it still feels that way.*

ORDER INFORMATION

To order additional copies of this book, please visit
www.redemption-press.com.
Also available on Amazon.com and BarnesandNoble.com
or by calling toll-free 1-844-2REDEEM.